THE GREAT DEFENDER

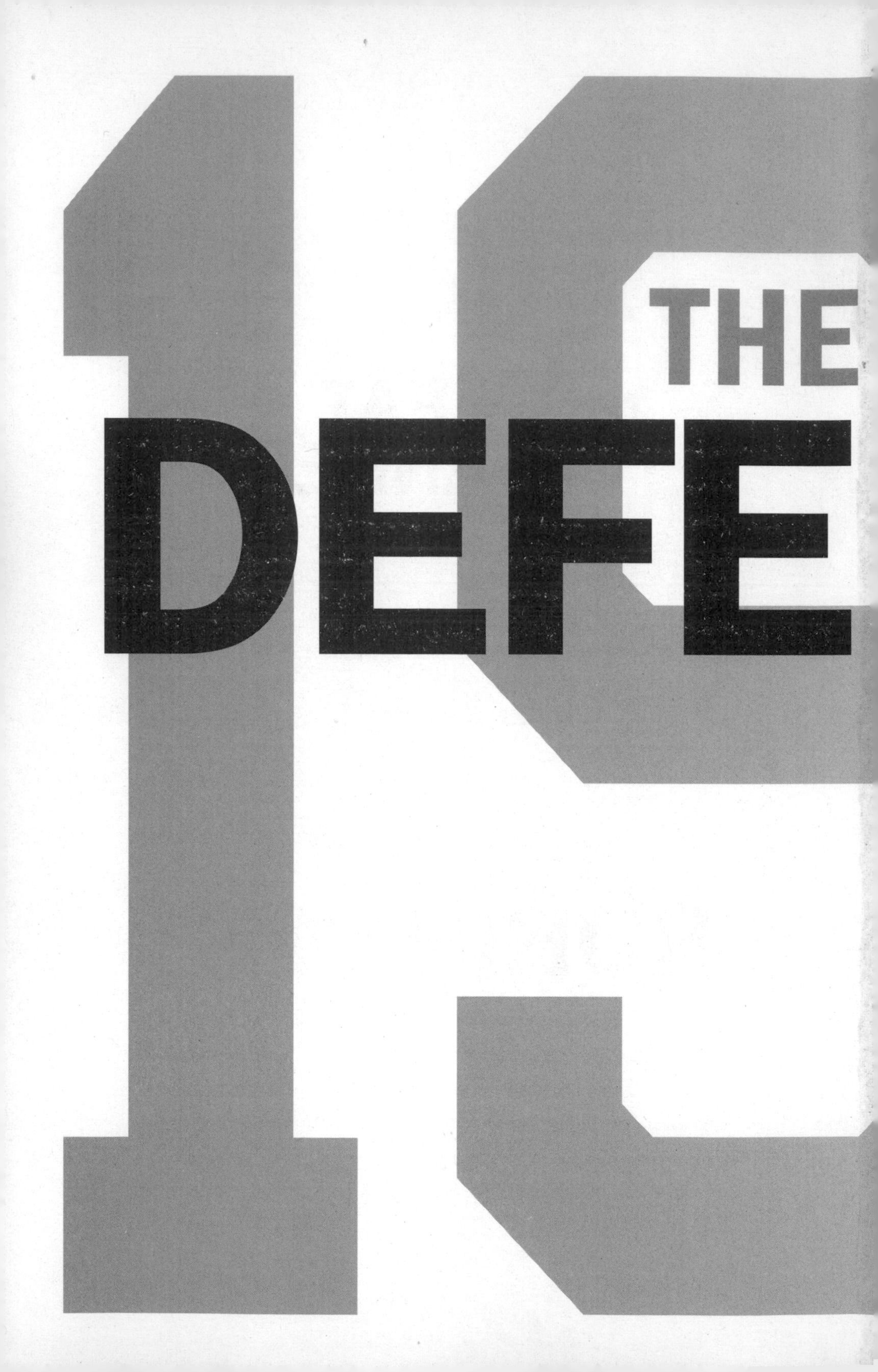
THE
DEFE

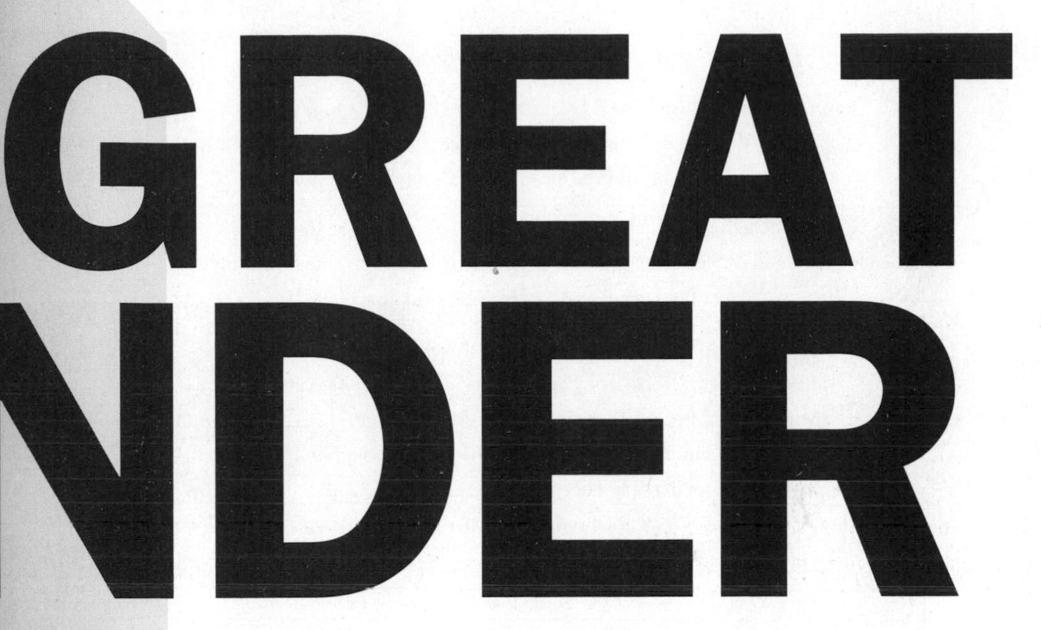

MY HOCKEY ODYSSEY

LARRY ROBINSON

with **KEVIN SHEA**

Fenn/McClelland & Stewart is an imprint of McClelland & Stewart,
a division of Random House of Canada Limited,
a Penguin Random House Company

Fenn/McClelland & Stewart and colophon are registered trademarks
of McClelland & Stewart, a division of Random House of Canada Limited,
a Penguin Random House Company

Library and Archives of Canada Cataloguing in Publication

ISBN: 978-0-7710-7236-9
ebook ISBN: 978-0-7710-7237-6

Published simultaneously in the United States of America by
McClelland & Stewart, a division of Random House of Canada Limited

Library of Congress Control Number available upon request

Printed and bound in the United States of America

McClelland & Stewart,
a division of Random House of Canada Limited,
a Penguin Random House Company
www.randomhouse.ca

1 2 3 4 5 18 17 16 15 14

I dedicate this book to my wife, Jeannette,
my two kids and three grandkids, as well as all family,
friends, and teammates who have made
telling this story possible.

CONTENTS

CHAPTER 1

The Great Defender

May 11, 1976.

Game Two of the 1976 Stanley Cup final.

The Montreal Canadiens hosted the defending Stanley Cup champion Philadelphia Flyers, who had brawled their way to celebrations in 1974 and 1975.

They wouldn't win a third.

The Flyers thought the way they were going to beat us was the same way they won the Cup the previous two years—through intimidation. They had 118 points during the regular season, but we finished with 127. We had a better team than the Flyers that year.

Gary Dornhoefer was one of those pests who got under the skin of a lot of teams, including the Canadiens. He was forever in front of the net, banging and crashing the crease, distracting Kenny Dryden. It wasn't that he was particularly big, but he was fearless. He added that extra dimension to the Flyers' lineup.

In the third period, just past the halfway mark, Dornhoefer took off, lugging the puck up the boards in the neutral zone. I was skating backwards and had read where the puck was going, so I angled towards him, readying a hip check, kind of lying in wait. As he took a stride, thinking he could beat me, I accelerated and hit him hard into the boards with my shoulder. We were both going at full speed, and the force of the collision caused us both to crash to the ice. The play was whistled dead, and when I got to my feet I saw a member of the maintenance crew shuffling across the ice. I wondered what he was doing as he went over with a hammer and started working on the boards. It turned out that the force of the hit had caused one of the supports to come loose and the boards were indented a couple of inches. They stopped the game for a few minutes while he tried to bang everything back into place.

"It was the best body check I've ever seen," stated broadcaster Bob Miller, shaking his head in amazement.

"It's the hardest I've ever been hit," admitted Dornhoefer.

I've spoken to Gary since then, and he told me he was spitting up blood after the game—and every bone in his body hurt.

I remember the check, but it wasn't until an event probably 15 or 16 years later that I actually watched it for the first time. I generally didn't like to watch myself on the ice because I was very hard on myself.

You're not necessarily looking for the hit, but when there's an opportunity, you take it. That was my chance. The club needed a lift.

He had done it with crushing ease. Just simple "aw shucks" destruction; the kind that leaves behind the shuddering hint of something more to come. He had delivered a message—to the Flyers, to the league, to himself.

It was the watershed moment of the series. The Canadiens won that game 2–1, and went on to sweep the reigning champions. The Broad Street Bullies had finally been brought down to earth: the intimidators became the intimidated. The reign of the Flyers came to a halt, and the start of a dynasty in Montreal had begun.

All the pieces had finally fallen into place. [Larry] had found his game—a game of strength and agility, a commanding mix of offence and defence; his size a lingering reminder of violence. In the next few years, more than just an outstanding player, Robinson became a presence.

—Ken Dryden, *The Game*

•

It is nearly impossible to select a definitive moment for any hockey player, but for someone like Larry Robinson, the chore becomes even more challenging when you consider the collection of highlights from his extraordinary 20-season NHL career, plus his subsequent career coaching at hockey's most elite level.

Consider this: Robinson is a six-time Stanley Cup champion, all with the Canadiens, and he won the Conn Smythe Trophy as the most valuable playoff performer in 1978. Not once during his 20 seasons in the NHL did a team on which he played fail to participate in postseason action, a record equalled only recently by Nicklas Lidstrom of the Red Wings. Robinson was twice the recipient of the Norris Trophy as the league's premier defenceman, and he played in the NHL All-Star Game on ten occasions.

He was equally dominant on the world stage, earning gold medals with Team Canada at the Canada Cup championships of 1976, 1981, and 1984. He was also named Best Defenceman at the 1981 World Championships in Sweden.

His coaching career includes three additional Stanley Cup championships, all with the New Jersey Devils.

But it is in Montreal where he is remembered best, and to celebrate the 75th anniversary of the franchise in 1984, the Canadiens revealed their all-time "dream team." Coached by Toe Blake, the team included goaltender Jacques Plante; forwards Jean Béliveau, Dickie Moore, and Maurice Richard; and, paired on the blue line, Doug Harvey and Larry Robinson. Journalist Red Fisher, who covered the team from 1954 to 2012, rated his top ten Canadiens of the last half-century, placing Robinson at number six behind legends Jean Béliveau, Maurice Richard, Guy Lafleur, Doug Harvey, and Henri Richard. Robinson was elected to the Hockey Hall of Fame in 1995, and in 2007 his number 19 was retired by the Montreal Canadiens.

This book chronicles the wonderful life and sensational career of "The Great Defender," Larry Robinson, in his own words.

CHAPTER 2

Marvellous Childhood in Marvelville

"Forget about him being one of the greatest players to have ever played the game, Larry is one of the greatest people I've ever met in my life." – DOUG WILSON (in *The Hockey News: Top 100 Players of All-Time by Position*)

To really understand me, you have to get a sense of where I come from. Even though I lived in two of the most cosmopolitan cities in the world when I was playing—Montreal and Los Angeles—I am a farm boy at heart. The values and work ethic I was raised with are deeply ingrained in me.

I am the third of five children born to Leslie James Robinson and Isobel (MacDonald) Robinson. We lost Mom in 1999, and Dad died in 2004.

I was born Larry Clark Robinson on June 2, 1951. My hometown of Marvelville is too small to have its own hospital, so like most others in our community, I was born at the Winchester District Memorial Hospital.

My oldest brother, Brian, died in 2005 at the age of 57 from a blood cancer called multiple myeloma. He went through the process of having a bone marrow transplant and was in remission for close to a year, but then the cancer returned and he passed away within three months. Brian was my big brother. I idolized him and, as a kid, often found myself tagging along with him and his friends. My eldest sister, Carol, moved out west to Hanna, Alberta, after she graduated from high school. She married a local guy from back home in Marvelville, and now they are recently retired in Olds, Alberta. My younger sister, Linda, lives in Ottawa. The youngest of us, my brother Morris—or Moe—was a hockey player, too. He briefly played with the Canadiens.

Mom and Dad were both from the Ottawa Valley and met there. Their entire life, really, was spent in the same 20-mile radius around our farm in Marvelville, Ontario, a small community about a 45-minute drive southeast of Ottawa. When I was growing up, the population was about 60. I like to joke that the sign that says, "You are now leaving Marvelville" is on the other side of the "Welcome to Marvelville" sign, but it's not so far from the truth. There isn't much there beyond farms and fields.

Marvelville was created because the rural community needed a postal address. The local general store had a post office, and my grandfather named the community Marvelville. Years ago, the general store got converted into apartments. The church is gone, too, and there's now a house there.

In 1998, Marvelville was absorbed into the newly created Township of North Dundas, the result of the amalgamation of the former Townships of Winchester and Mountain and the Villages of Chesterville and Winchester.

Our dairy farm sat on a couple of hundred acres, and we had 55 or 60 head of cattle during the summer and about 25 in the winter. Besides the cattle, we also had horses and chickens, and we grew corn and hay. We all grew up working hard: there is always a lot of work to be done on a farm no matter how old you are. I started driving the tractor in the fields at the age of seven, and Dad had to put a block of wood on the clutch so I could reach it and change the gears. I was driving a tractor three years before I ever milked a cow.

Dad would come into our room about six o'clock each morning, and our day began with, "Okay boys, time to get up." We had to get our chores done, and then get inside and eat our breakfast before walking to school. When we were in high school, the school bus picked us up at 7:20. Our chores began with feeding the calves and cattle, and then we'd open the gates and start milking the cows, which had to be done twice a day. The calves would get their mother's milk for the first week and a half to two weeks, but after that, because we were in the dairy business, we'd mix the milk with powdered milk for them. Another of my jobs was to climb up the silo and throw the silage down: the smell was awful, and it got in your hair and clothes and would stay with you all day. We'd also have to put down the hay for the cattle, feed them, and clean the gutters. We had chickens, too, so we used to collect the eggs, and later we would peddle eggs in and around Ottawa.

We also grew crops on the farm. My dad's brother Ray lived next door to us, so we shared tractors and helped each other plant in the spring and take the hay off in the fall. Come summertime, between the two farms we'd put in close to 12,000 bales. It's not like today, where everything is done by machine, from putting the hay in big rolls to picking them up and stacking them. Everything was done by hand back then. The hay would be collected and we'd have to stack those heavy bales really high in the silos. One of us would put the bales on the elevators and two others would be at the top, piling them as high as possible. We'd pile nine hundred or a thousand bales in those silos to last the cattle through the year.

While the boys were outside, the girls did most of the household chores, cooking and cleaning. We ran the farm as a family for years. I left home to play hockey when I was 17 years old, and eventually Brian bought the farm from Dad and took it over. Mom and Dad moved to Metcalfe, and Brian worked the farm for five or six years before selling off much of the land in the late '70s to a Dutch family down the road from us. Brian and his family lived on what was left of the original Robinson farm, and since his death, his oldest son continues to call it home.

When you're raised on a farm, your values are a lot different than if you were raised in the city. It's likely because more of your time is occupied. I think a lot of kids today get into trouble because they don't have anything else to do, so they get into mischief and hang out with the wrong people. We were good kids. Oh, we did mischievous things—we could be rascals—but we never did anything really harmful. On Hallowe'en, for example, my older brother and a couple of his friends would drive around and steal mailboxes and then dump them in the ditch. One time, we took an old horse carriage belonging to my uncle and put it on his front porch. Like a lot of kids, we would put cow manure in a paper bag, light the bag on fire, and put it on someone's porch, then ring the doorbell and run like hell. The people would come out and try to stomp out the fire and get their shoes covered in manure. We did stuff like that.

Farm life also gave us a unique perspective. When my son Jeffery was young, we were at Mom and Dad's farm, and I thought it would be good to have him witness a calf being born. I explained that if the cow was having difficulty, someone had to help with the birth. In this case, the calf was beginning to come, but there were some problems—the front legs came out first and I had to tie a rope around the calf's front legs to help pull it free. After a great deal of struggling, the calf finally emerged. I'll never forget Jeffery's comment: "Dad, after all the trouble the calf had getting out of there, I'll bet he never goes back in there again."

Animals played an important role in our lives. Not only were they our family's livelihood, but we had many as pets through the years. One of the reasons I later got into polo was because we always had a horse at the farm, and if we didn't have one, our uncle next door had one. We loved to go on trail rides at the local Circle J Ranch. As part of the 4-H Club, we had to raise our own calf and take it to the local fair in September. We also had hundreds of cats through the years, especially to keep the mice population down. And we *always* had a dog.

We had a collie named Lassie that I really loved. Lassie was beautiful and incredibly well trained. If a cow calved and was in the far corner of our property, Lassie could be sent to bring the calf and the cow back to the barn by himself. After our milking was done, our cows would be taken down the road, past my uncle's farm, to a pasture about two miles away. Most of the fields around our farm were either in oats or corn or hay, so that's why we took the cattle to that pasture. There was far more grass for them there, and the cows habitually knew the way. I was ten years old, and I'd take the tractor to follow the cows and make sure that they got there, and then I'd close the gate.

But one time, Lassie slid under the tractor tire and I didn't see him, and when I backed up, I backed over him. My uncle saw what had happened and came running over to tell me. I cried like a baby! That was the worst thing that ever happened to me. I was only ten, but it still haunts me. We had other dogs after that, but they were nowhere near as well trained as Lassie. He was a special dog.

All of us kids attended U.S.S. (Union School Section) No. 5 Russell, a one-room schoolhouse on Gregoire Road that had maybe 25 or 30 students each year, covering all grades from one through eight. A busy grade might have had five or six kids in it. I'd say 15 or 20 per cent of the school came from two families, with six or seven kids each. My teacher for Grades 1 through 3 was Flora Fader, and then up to Grade 8 I had Graham Marcellus. When we were kids, the school seemed miles and miles away, but you could actually jog there in two minutes. The school closed in 1965, and then we were bused to another school in Russell. Today, U.S.S. No. 5 Russell is the Marvelville Community Centre, and it's the only public building in town. My brother Moe lives right next door to it, and the community centre has a few artifacts from my career on display.

After Grade 8, I attended Osgoode Township High School. It was quite a change from our one-room elementary school, even though there were only 300 students. When I was there in Grade 9, there was no gym, although one was built by the time I started Grade 10.

I was a good student, and did well in math. For some reason, I was always able to remember numbers. For example, we had an old crank phone back then, and our phone number was 21-ring 2. I was good in most subjects that didn't require reading, because I couldn't keep my concentration for that long; I wanted to get up and get moving. If I had put more work into my studies and worked a little bit harder, I could have done much better, but sports just took over my life and I was out of school after Grade 11. I finished some of my Grade 12 taking correspondence courses during my first year as a pro, but I'm still a few credits short of my high school diploma. Maybe one of these days I'll complete it just for fun, but at the time, sports was a little more important—and then I had to try to make a living and support a young family.

Outside of school and work on the farm, we got involved in a lot of other things that kept us busy, like the 4-H program, which taught life and leadership skills to farm kids. I also loved music—I always wanted to sing in a band in high school but never got the chance (not that I had a good voice or anything). We all took piano lessons when we were young, and I can remember playing "The Lincolnshire Poacher" in a concert. We also took accordion lessons and guitar lessons. I can't play any of them, but we dabbled in them all. The problem always was that I just never spent enough time at one thing. I'd much rather have been outdoors doing sports.

We played the usual childhood games like kick the can and hide-and-go-seek. All the neighbours would end up at our place for some reason, and we had some really, really good friends. In fact, I was around 12 when I found out that we weren't even related to them—they were just friends that we had gathered over the years. Like our family, the Godwins had five kids, and we were all about the same age. There were two older boys, Howie and Teddy, an older sister, Betty, and two younger kids, Raymond and Gordie. We used to spend a lot of time together. Sometimes we'd go to bed and there'd be four kids in the room, and we'd wake to find *eight* kids in the room. They used to like to hang around at our house, and would help us at hay time and harvest time.

We played every sport as kids. I had really sprouted once I started high school, and was keen to join every team that would have me. When it was football season, I played tight end and linebacker. We only had 500 students in our school, so we didn't have enough guys to field both an offensive and a defensive squad, and about three-quarters of our team played both ways. In Grade 12, not only did our team go undefeated, but we didn't surrender a single point all the way through the regular season. We also had only seven points scored against us in an exhibition game with Ashbury College, a private boys' boarding school in Ottawa where Bobby Simpson, who played for the Ottawa Rough Riders, was the coach following his retirement. He called the game after five minutes because a fight broke out (our little high school team kicked their butts and they didn't like it), and it ended up being the only seven points we had scored against us that season. I actually could have been drafted by the Ottawa Rough Riders myself, but I chose hockey instead.

We played a lot of baseball, too, including a game called "strike-out," where one kid would be stand up at bat in front of the garage while another one would pitch. If the pitcher threw three strikes, then you switched around and the other kid pitched. In real baseball, my brother Brian used to catch for me—I was usually the pitcher. In the early years, until I got into senior ball, I probably pitched two or three games every weekend—Friday night, sometimes two games on Saturday, and then another game on Sunday. I threw my arm out after a few years.

I was never a singles hitter. I was a long-ball hitter with power to the opposite field. If the pitcher threw me a changeup, I was often waiting on it and would try to crush it the other way.

Softball was huge in our area, too. Between our family, my cousins next door, and the addition of a couple of neighbours, there were always enough of us to put together a Marvelville softball team. When I got older, I played on some really good softball teams in the Ottawa area—one that almost represented Canada at a tournament in New Zealand. We unfortunately lost 2–1 to Oshawa in a game that went 12 innings.

I was still playing senior softball in my early years with the Canadiens. One summer, I'll bet we played a schedule of close to 60 games—*after* I had played over a hundred games in the NHL. As a matter of fact, the Canadiens had a softball team of their own that travelled all over Quebec during the summer, playing charity games.

I enjoyed track and field, too, and competed in most of the events. I did competed in the long jump and triple jump, ran in relays, and did the shot put and discus throw. At one time, I held a number of track records for our high school.

I also played basketball, and we were the provincial high school basketball champions when I was in Grade 10. It seemed I was always one of the taller kids in my grade. Dad was six foot three, and I grew to be just under six foot four. I am the tallest of my brothers (Brian was about six-two and Moe is about six-three), and my sisters are a little above average in height. My growth spurt really took place in my first year of high school, which coincided with my entering a number of competitive sports. I grew three inches in Grade 9, and that really sprouted me up.

One summer, I was chosen along with one of the girls in my high school to attend an athletic leadership camp in Toronto. We learned almost every sport as well as coaching. Our school excelled in athletics in spite of itself. We didn't get the top-flight coaching that kids get today; in fact, we were practically self-taught. Our coaches were volunteers. Our geography teacher was one of our football coaches and our gym teacher was our track and field coach.

Hockey has always been a part of my life, going back as far as I can remember. We used to play a lot of ball hockey in the barn. The inside walls of the barn used to be whitewashed in order to keep everything fairly sterile, because we were working with milk. Apparently, that killed most of the germs. Dad used to get ticked off at us because every time we'd bang our sticks, the whitewash would crumble to the floor. Brian was a good hockey player, but just not passionate about it the way Moe and I were.

Every Saturday night, my mom, dad, and us boys sat together for our weekly tradition: *Hockey Night in Canada*. The girls didn't watch a lot of hockey—they'd be off playing with their dolls—but we'd sit in our pyjamas, eating toast and drinking cocoa while we watched the games on a big old black-and-white television set. There was no cable at the time, so we had a huge antenna outside the house. Where we lived, we could watch the Maple Leafs, but we could also get CBFT from Montreal, so we saw the Canadiens games too, although the play-by-play was in French with René Lecavalier. There was a French family, the Martells, who lived down the road from us, and we picked up a little bit of French from them, but we were also taking it in school, so we could watch the games in French and have a pretty good idea what was going on. I never *really* learned the language until I moved to Montreal and was playing for the Canadiens, however. I did a lot of interviews in French and even did a few commercials. I still can converse pretty well in French today, although I'm a little rusty.

Even though Toronto was always on *Hockey Night in Canada*, my favourite team was the Chicago Black Hawks. I loved their sweaters, and our minor hockey league team wore Black Hawk jerseys too (although I recently found a picture of me at about 12 years of age wearing a Montreal Canadiens sweater). Back then, the Chicago Black Hawks seldom won, but that's why I liked them—they were the underdogs. I didn't really like Montreal, actually, because they won all the time. Finally, in the early '60s, Chicago really came on and had a great team, winning the Stanley Cup in 1961.

I liked Stan Mikita and Pierre Pilote, but Bobby Hull was my favourite. Pierre wasn't really physical. He wouldn't beat a lot of players with his speed, either, but he was a heady player and was fun to watch. Mikita was great and very tough. But Bobby Hull was just so exciting. He would wind up and, from behind his own net, skate the length of the ice, and then wind up with that warped blade and let a slapshot fly. I got the chance to play with Bobby at the Canada Cup in 1976, and when I was playing with the Los Angeles Kings, there was a Canadian Club in L.A. that organized a banquet to honour me after my retirement. They brought in Bobby to speak at it, and gave me a Chicago Blackhawks sweater with my name on the back that I still have.

Marvelville sure wasn't Chicago, and growing up on a farm in a small community didn't provide the same excitement that some of my friends who grew up in large cities enjoyed, but it gave me a very strong work ethic, a love of athletics, and prepared me well for life in the National Hockey League.

CHAPTER 3

Playing on the Ponds

"You always reminisce with great fondness about where you've been and what you've done. You remember the days when you were on the pond with a couple of friends. You never forget your roots." – LARRY ROBINSON

We Robinson kids lived on our skates. I had a hand-me-down pair that had belonged to my brother Brian, and they were several sizes too big for me, but that didn't stop me; I just wore two or three pairs of thick socks to make them fit better.

My uncle Ray and his family lived next to us in Marvelville. They had a big pond behind their house, and when I was four years old and first learning to skate, we'd take old wooden chairs out onto the ice and lean on them as we pushed them along. Then, once we got our balance, we'd push the chair out of the way, and lo and behold, we were skating on our own—although in the early days, we spent as much time on our butts as we did on our blades. But that's how we all learned.

There was also a little pond down below our own house, where we would clean off the ice and skate. There was a small creek that ran in back of our house as well, and that was the most fun. It would be 20 below, but we didn't care. I can remember the squeak of the snow as we walked and the creak of the icy branches of the overhanging trees. We'd get on the ice before the snow fell and see just how far we could go. There'd be times when you'd have to traverse off because you ran into a spring or something and you didn't want to fall through the ice. Otherwise, we'd skate for miles and miles and miles and then head back home for lunch. We wouldn't even take our skates off, just wolf down a sandwich and a glass of milk and then head back out for more.

There was always an outdoor rink built at our school every year, too. My brother Brian and I, plus a couple of local kids, would get the key to the school from the corner store, unlock the place and start working on the rink. We'd have to water the snow so that it would be flat and smooth: one guy would wet the snow and everybody else would tramp on it until we got a little foundation that would hold water. There was a pipe that went underground from the school to a corner of the ice rink, and we'd take turns flooding the rink through the night. One of my uncles had an old flight suit that he'd worn when he was in the air force. One guy would go out in the suit for about an hour until he couldn't feel his hands anymore, and then he'd come in and another guy would take a turn. When our shift would finish, we'd go inside the school, play cards, get warm, and maybe sleep a bit, waiting for our next shift. By morning, there'd be a beautiful sheet of virgin ice, and we'd pull on our skates and play hockey.

I was the youngest in the group, so you can guess who had to play goal all the time. The worst part was having to stand in one place for so long. After a while, you could barely feel your feet, and inevitably, the play would come down into our end and one of the boys would shoot the puck and hit you in the foot. You'd swear your foot was going to fall off!

There was an annual local carnival that would take place at the rink. The biggest events were the races, and you'd do everything you could to be the fastest skater. We simply learned to skate through trial and error. It was nothing like the kids have now. Today, they would have somebody out there coaching them on using both the inside and outside edges of their skates, for instance. I think kids today have as much fun as we did, but I also think we have a tendency to teach too much these days—especially when the kids are young and just starting out. "You go stand here and you go stand there. Hold your stick this way." That kind of stuff.

When my son was first learning to skate, I used to take him down to the local rink in Kirkland when the Canadiens weren't practising. They would divide the rink into three sections, and they just put 10 or 12 kids out there on the ice, threw a puck in the middle, and just let them play. I loved it so much. It was hilarious watching the kids. They'd run into each other and just get up and go after the puck again. They'd all chase after the puck with their short, choppy little strides, leaning on their sticks for support. It was just about getting out there and having some fun. That's what's missing in our young kids' game today.

I played my first organized hockey when Brian and I registered to play in a minor hockey league sponsored by the local Lions Club in Russell. Brian was 12 at the time and I was eight. I was put onto a peewee team.

Minor hockey relies so much on its volunteers, and in Russell, one of the biggest supporters was Dr. Frank Kinnaird, our family doctor. When parents were unable to take time off work to drive their kids to games and tournaments, Dr. Kinnaird would do it. That arena in Russell where we played has since been renamed the Dr. Kinnaird Arena. As hockey took more and more of a hold on my life, Dad reorganized some of our schedule to accommodate games and practices. Occasionally, he'd let me off the hook and do the chores himself.

We simply loved to play, but that year, we had a really good team and only lost a couple of games. Carson McVey and I were two of the better players, and we often got invited to play with the older guys. I mostly played centre, but I was put on defence at times, which meant I got to stay on the ice even more. We only had two lines and a couple of spares, and I think we only carried two or three defencemen, so I probably played 45 or 50 minutes a game. I loved it.

I was 12 before I got my first pair of new skates. While we had always had a very successful team, it was around that age that we won the natural ice championship. Then we faced Cornwall, who were the artificial ice champions, in their own arena. I remember looking around: it seemed to me like there were 100,000 people in the stands, but it was more like 1,800. It didn't matter. It was the largest crowd I had ever played in front of at that time. We ended up beating them 2–1 in the final. Our coach, Bill Linegar, was a great guy and another one of those locals who did so much for the area. Unfortunately, one weekend, his car skidded out of control going around a corner and he was killed. That was a huge loss for our community. Bill was a special guy for a lot of young kids who were playing hockey at the time.

Another year, we were involved in a tournament that included a team from Thurso, Quebec, who had a hotshot kid named Guy Lafleur. Even then, he was amazing. Thurso beat us badly and Guy scored most of their goals, including one on a slapshot all the way from centre. There was little we could do to defend against him, and I was glad to have him on *my* team later.

When I played defence back then, I was really an offensive defenceman. I could skate backwards pretty well and had good peripheral vision, but if I had a problem, it was getting caught up the ice too often. Until Bobby Orr came along, defencemen just didn't carry the puck that much. It was the defenceman's job to stay back and just pass the puck forward. Bobby Orr opened the door for all of us to become more offensive.

Before Bobby Orr, Pierre Pilote was a bit of a rushing defenceman, but he was a lot smaller so he wasn't as physical. He was more like Brad Park, who wouldn't beat a lot of people with speed or finesse, but both he and Pilote really used their heads. Pierre Pilote was one of my favourites to watch, being a Chicago Black Hawks fan.

I had a number of hockey heroes, but the very first autograph I ever got was from Red Kelly. He was our guest speaker at a year-end hockey banquet in Russell. Red had been an all-star defenceman with the Detroit Red Wings, but was converted to a centre when he joined the Toronto Maple Leafs. I reminded Red that he signed the first autograph I ever collected, and we have a good laugh about that when I see him at Hockey Hall of Fame functions.

Another year, Ron Ellis came as a guest speaker. I was in awe of these NHL players; they took the time to talk to us about careers in hockey. Both Pilote and Ellis were so polite and made sure that every one of us got an autograph. That rubbed off on me even back then. I remember how I felt when I met a hockey hero, and I've always made certain that I sign everything I'm asked to sign and pose for every picture that a fan asks for.

CHAPTER 4

Junior Achievement

"Larry's got a long reach, has great puck-carrying ability and is an excellent skater for a big man. He's as rough as he has to be. And he's smart. He needs some polish to become an NHLer. He's got all the things he needs to become a National Hockey League star." – AL MACNEIL (in *The Hockey News*)

When I was playing with the Metcalfe Jets of the St. Lawrence Junior B League, we had a coach named Irwin Duncan. Irwin and his twin brother, Edwin, were from Vernon, Ontario, near my hometown, and in the 1940s they played junior together with the Inkerman Rockets of the Central Ottawa Valley Junior Hockey League. A year or so after the Duncan boys were there, Hall of Famer Leo Boivin and broadcaster Brian McFarlane also played on that team.

I was only 14, but was a pretty good skater, so Irwin had me playing centre. His son Alan was on my wing, but we didn't play a lot because the other players on the team were so much older and bigger than us. Irwin Duncan taught us a lot about positional hockey—what to do and where to be. He later told the *Ottawa Citizen*, "Larry had it all. He was so big and strong and he could skate. He was a wonderful kid to coach; always in good spirits. Do anything you asked." That was a great start for my career.

Geographically, we fell within the territory of the Ottawa 67's, a brand new Junior A franchise in the Ontario Hockey Association that was keeping its eye on teams in the area. Several years later, I found out that Bill Long, who had been hired as Ottawa's first coach and GM, knew about me, but didn't think I had what it takes to be a hockey player. I never did get an invitation to play junior in Ottawa. But Norm Baril, GM of the Cornwall Royals, a Tier II junior team, invited three of us from Metcalfe—Alan Duncan, Carson McVeigh, and me—to their training camp. Right after the first practice, Norm came over to the three of us. We all had long hair, which was the style at the time. "I want you guys to go into this room," he said, pointing to a door down the hall. The three of us walked into the room, and there was a guy there who shaved off all of our hair. Norm then said, "Okay, now you guys are ready to play for our team."

We all went home. "Dad, I'm not going back there," I fumed. "That's it. I don't want to play with them anymore."

In the meantime, as it turned out, I got a call from the Ottawa 67's Junior B team. They were going to be playing Cornwall and invited me to join them. My dad and I jumped into the car, but on our way there, we ran into a frigging snowstorm. By the time we got to the game, the first period was almost over. The coach shrugged. "Oh well. Too late now," he said. "Why don't you just sit and watch the game?"

While I was sitting there, a scout named Barry Fraser came over and started talking to my dad. Barry would go on to help build the Edmonton Oilers' dynasty as their director of scouting, but back then, he was working with the Brockville Braves. Through my father, he invited me to go to their Junior A camp in Athens, just outside Brockville. "If you bring your son up here and he makes the team, I'll owe you a bottle of rye whiskey," he promised, rye being what my dad drank.

I did go to Athens for their training camp, and the coach, Dan Dexter, liked my skating and my size and thought playing defence would be a better fit for me. Truth be told, Brockville had only two defencemen, so they needed another guy back on the blue line anyhow. But Dan was the one who taught me how to *really* play defence, and that's basically where my career took off. I made their team and ended up playing junior for the Brockville Braves of the Central Junior A Hockey League in 1968–69.

•

A new family moved into Marvelville when I was in high school. The Lamirandes rented a farm just down the road from ours. Gerald Lamirande was a retired corporal in the Royal Canadian Air Force and had always wanted to live on a farm. After he retired, the Lamirandes did just that. The family included six daughters and one son, and word got around pretty quickly that a lot of cute girls had just moved into the area.

My buddy Teddy Godwin and I were on our way back from town and we saw the lights on at the Lamirande place. As we got closer, we could hear that there was a party going on, so we decided to stop by. One of the daughters, Jeannette, was initially upset that we crashed the party, but we ended up meeting the family and I got to meet all of the girls.

Originally, I kind of liked Jeannette's sister, Pauline. Her brother, Gerry, was a hockey fan, and he would drag Jeannette and an older sister, Nicole, to my games. I had a girlfriend at the time, but I really hit it off with Jeannette, who had just broken up with her boyfriend. We started spending time together, and the next thing we knew, we were inseparable.

I wanted to stay in school in Osgoode Township so I could play football. If I went to school in Brockville, they wouldn't let me play, but that meant that I had to drive to hockey practice every day. My dad bought me my very first car, a 1964 Pontiac that had sat abandoned in a field for a year. It cost only $400, but Dad put a battery in it and it started right up. I drove it home and spent all day cleaning it, polishing it, and waxing it.

I picked up Jeannette and we were on our way to Brockville for practice, but just before we arrived at the arena, a guy who'd been drinking with six people in the car hit me broadside. It spun the Pontiac around 360 degrees and damaged it really badly. By the time it stopped spinning, I was sure that it was totalled. Luckily, Jeannette was sitting close to me on the bench seat: the guy hit me on the passenger side, and had she been sitting close to the door, she might have been badly hurt. I have no doubt that if I had had a smaller car, we would have been killed.

The guy got out of his car and started yelling at me. "What are you doing?" I glared at him and barked, "This is my first car. Get your fucking ass back in that car before I beat the shit out of you. I'm going to call the cops!"

The guy turned white and went back and sat in his car, waiting for the police to come. I phoned my dad, and he came and met us. I used Dad's car so that Jeannette and I could go to the practice while Dad waited for our neighbour, who owned the insurance company and would put through the claim to get my car repaired.

The car had 70,000 miles on it, and I ended up driving it for over 100,000 miles myself. Then Moe and my mother drove it, and

I think by the time they retired it, it had about 220,000 miles on it. It didn't owe us a dime, and it saved our lives.

We had some real characters on that team in Brockville. There were three guys from Newfoundland who were completely wild but really good hockey players: Alex Blanchard was a centre, Craig Bugden played defence, and Jimmy Duhart was a left winger. Funny enough, I introduced Jeannette's sister Nicole to Jimmy, and they ended up getting married. We had a couple of great defencemen. Dan Creighton was an all-star in 1968–69 and Steve Bajinski went on to play at Cornell University. Our coach, Dan Dexter, had played U.S. college hockey at Clarkson.

I had been one of the bigger guys on the teams I played on from the time I was in bantam, and when that's the case, you stick up for the smaller guys that teams try to take advantage of. I ended up having some real battles. One was against the Oshawa Generals. Brockville was a Tier II junior team, while the Generals were in the OHA's Junior A league, and when they came up to play an exhibition game, they thought they could rough us up. We weren't going to be pushed around. Steve Bajinski fought Bob Kelly, who went on to play with the Broad Street Bullies in Philadelphia, and was really giving it to him. Ivan Boldirev, who went on to play with a bunch of teams, including the Chicago Black Hawks and Vancouver Canucks, tried to jump in. I caught him before he could get involved, and he and I really started throwing punches. He was a couple of years older than I was, but all I knew was that I was going to keep swinging as hard as I could for as long as I could. It was a pretty good battle. Their coach, Ike Hildebrand, called the game because we were kicking their asses and he didn't want his guys to get hurt.

We finished fourth in the league in 1968–69, but lost to the Hull Castors in the semifinals, where I had another battle. Hull had this big kid, John Coburn, and we started slugging each other in front of our net. By the time it was over, we were at the far blue line. Some of the boys back home still talk about that fight.

Hull moved on through the playoffs and added me to their team as a forward for a series against the Sorel Black Hawks of the Quebec Junior Hockey League. At that time, teams were allowed to choose three players from eliminated teams to join them in the next round. Sorel featured Dan Bouchard in goal, Michel Brière, and a guy I'd meet again in the NHL, Dave Schultz. Unfortunately, Sorel dumped us fairly easily to move on to the Memorial Cup eastern semifinal against the Montreal Junior Canadiens.

In 1969–70, I felt much more comfortable playing defence and was fortunate to be named to the league's First All-Star Team and be chosen the best defenceman. We finished second that season and faced the Smiths Falls Bears in the semifinals. They had a tough guy named Dave McFadden: a big, six-foot, two-inch monster on skates. At one point, McFadden stood in front of our bench and challenged any one of us to come over the boards and take him on. I couldn't resist, and was likely the only guy on our team who would dare go up against him. We went toe to toe. It was a good scrap. I don't think either of us won the decision, but I showed him and the Bears that we weren't going to be intimidated. We ended up eliminating Smiths Falls, but lost in the final against Ottawa M&W Rangers.

I was flattered that Ottawa asked Brockville to loan me, Alan Duncan, and Gerry Teeple to their team for their series against Hilliard Graves and the Charlottetown Mariners of the Maritime Junior A Hockey League. I ended up playing forward, but we got our asses kicked. I really believe that had Brockville played the Mariners, we might have stood a chance—Brockville had a tougher team. As it was, I ended up having to do all the fighting for everybody and Charlottetown basically just intimidated our team.

But those were really great days. A few years ago, I was honoured when the Brockville Braves retired my number 3. The CJHL now has two divisions: one is named after Stevie Yzerman, who played for the Nepean Raiders before he joined the Red Wings, and they named the other division after me.

•

Barry Fraser ended up leaving Brockville to join the Kitchener Rangers, and he invited me to their camp prior to the 1970–71 season. Wouldn't you know, it was just at that time that I found out that Jeannette was pregnant. We had been dating for a while and definitely loved each other, but certainly had no plans to start a family at that time. We were both still teenagers with uncertain futures, and it was the last thing we needed in our lives at that time—but we accepted the responsibility and decided that we would get married and figure things out as we went along.

We were so frigging busy, though. In a farm household, there are always so many things going on, and everybody has their own itinerary. I was trying to find the right time to tell my parents the news. Finally, I simply left a note on the medicine cabinet in the bathroom. I figured that, sooner or later, somebody *had* to go to the bathroom!

That's how my mom and dad found out that they were going to become grandparents, and that Jeannette and I would soon be married. But during that summer of 1970, Mom and Dad had made plans to visit my oldest sister and her husband, who had moved out west to Hanna, Alberta, because he got a job with an oil company there. The problem was that my parents had already purchased their plane tickets and would have lost a fair bit of money to change their plans or to cancel altogether. So instead, Jeannette and I proceeded with our wedding with our good family friends, the Godwins, standing in for my parents.

It was a very small but nice ceremony arranged on short notice at the church in Metcalfe. I had been raised Protestant and Jeannette was Roman Catholic, so we had both a minister and a priest officiate at the wedding. Since then, I've taken my catechism and have become Catholic, and our kids have been raised Catholic as well.

After the ceremony, we went back to my parents' place and had a little party. But it wasn't so little in the end: the next morning, we got up and found people everywhere. There were people sleeping on the couch, on the floor, and in the basement. It sure made us smile!

We never did get the chance to go on a honeymoon. I've promised Jeannette that I'll make it up to her on our 50th wedding anniversary. I'd like to renew our vows then, too.

Jeannette and I were getting ready to move to Kitchener, and after Mom and Dad got back from out west, family and friends threw us a big going-away party at the Marvelville Community Centre. We had a fabulous time, and I must admit that I was pretty inebriated by the end of the night. Jeannette wasn't drinking at all because of the baby, which was due around the beginning of October. We got back home and I immediately fell into a deep sleep.

In the middle of the night, Jeannette woke me up. "Larry! Larry! My water broke!" Half asleep and still woozy from the party, I looked at her and mumbled, "What do you want me to do?" and then proceeded to roll over and fall back asleep.

Jeannette went to my parents' bedroom and got them up. They ran into our room and made sure I was up. We got a couple of neighbours to drive us to the hospital in Ottawa—our friends in the front and me with Jeannette in the back seat. Back then, husbands weren't allowed in the delivery room, so my friends and I went to a little restaurant nearby and I poured a cup of coffee down my throat before hurrying back, waiting to learn of the birth of our baby.

Jeffery was safely born on September 4, 1970, four weeks premature. He weighed just a little more than five pounds, and I could hold him in one hand. They had to keep him in an incubator at the hospital for an extra couple of weeks because his weight dropped down to four pounds, eleven ounces (he had to be five pounds before they would allow us to take him home). Then he ended up with some bronchitis. But while he wasn't a healthy baby at the time, he grew into a big, strong young man who drove us crazy. But he was beautiful, and it was an enormously emotional time for us.

Our lives certainly changed with Jeffery's arrival. A baby brings new responsibilities that were largely foreign to Jeannette and me. Sleep? What's that? But we wouldn't trade those days for anything. I instantaneously had to figure out how to juggle a junior career, support a family, and learn how to raise an infant.

When I moved to Kitchener, I had intended to take a trade course at school, but when Jeffery arrived, I had to take a job to support the family. Those were very difficult times; I don't even know how we made it through. I was making $60 a week playing junior with Kitchener, and Punch Scherer, the Rangers' general manager, got me a job with Kitchener Beverages, one of the team's sponsors. I'd have to be there at seven in the morning and we'd deliver cases of pop until 3:30 or 4:00. Then I'd go straight to the rink for a 4:30 practice, which lasted an hour or so, before heading home, exhausted. I think I made $200 a week at Kitchener Beverages, and we were paying about $150 a month for rent at the time.

The Rangers boarded their players, and Jeannette and I lived on the top floor of a house owned by a lady named Mrs. Vaillancourt, who lived with her brother and daughter. We really had no idea what we were doing as parents, so Mrs. Vaillancourt helped us immensely. She was especially great with Jeannette. And once in a while, she'd babysit Jeffery so we could go out, which we couldn't afford to do very often.

Back then, the Montreal Junior Canadiens played in the OHA, so a few times that season, we'd travel by bus and play the Ottawa 67's on Friday night and then the Junior Canadiens on Saturday. Right after the game, the bus would drive through the night to get back to Kitchener. I'd have a little time on Sunday, but it would be back to work on Monday morning.

We just kind of scraped by—I have to tell you, we ate a lot of Kraft Dinner. A big night for us was when I'd get selected as one of the three stars of the game, because they'd give us a free voucher to get some food at the local grocery store. We'd treat ourselves to some chicken wings and Baby Duck or something like that, but life back then certainly wasn't easy.

The Rangers were a pretty good team. Glen Seperich was our goaltender, and we had some skill up front with Billy Barber, Jerry Byers, Tom Cassidy, and Teddy Scharf. On defence, there was Chris Ahrens, Ralph Hopiavouri, Phil Iwaskiewicz, Gary Sproule, and me. I had the luxury of getting a lot of ice time: Chris Ahrens and I played 35 to 40 minutes a game, and I learned so much about playing the position that year. When the Rangers fired the coach, Jerry Forler, partway through the season, they hired Ron Murphy to take over. I'd learned a lot from Jerry, but Ron had played in the NHL, so we learned a lot from him, too.

We finished the regular season in sixth place, and who do we end up playing in the quarter-final but the frigging St. Catharines Black Hawks—so it was basically the Kitchener Rangers against their star, Marcel Dionne, who was an absolute powerhouse in the league. Every game went to overtime, but by the end of each game, Marcel had two or three goals, and we'd lose a close one. He was just dominant. We were swept by St. Catharines in four straight, and they went on to win our league championship against the Toronto Marlboros.

Still, I really enjoyed living in Kitchener. It was such a clean city, and people were very, very friendly and big supporters of the team. We always got great crowds there. Mom and Dad would also make the trek down every once in a while, and Jeanette's sister and her husband used to come to stay with us a lot of the time, so we had great family support. We also had some really good friends. My teammate Teddy Scharf and his wife, Ann, used to come over and help us out every once in a while, and we became very good friends with Billy Barber, too. His late wife was his girlfriend at the time, and we knew them very well.

After we were eliminated in the first round of the playoffs by Dionne's Black Hawks, Jeannette and I packed up our things and headed back home to Metcalfe to live with my parents for the summer—something we did until I made enough money to afford our own little place. (We finally ended up buying a cottage after the Stanley Cup win in 1973, and we made that our home.)

Back in Metcalfe, we needed to make some money, and Mom was more than happy to take on some of the responsibilities of looking after Jeffery. Jeannette got a job as a waitress in Ottawa and I went back to work on the family farm, wondering what was around the corner for my hockey career.

While that year was tough, I can reflect back on it with great satisfaction. Kitchener gave me the opportunity to take responsibility for my life and those of Jeannette and Jeffery. The Rangers also proved to be instrumental in my path to the NHL. I wore the number 3 while playing in Kitchener (I don't know whether it was because I liked Pierre Pilote, or if it was simply the sweater they handed me), but when I got to the NHL I wore the number 19. The Kitchener Rangers don't retire jersey numbers; instead, they honour certain numbers, and I am very proud to have number 19, the number I wore with the Canadiens, hanging from the rafters at the Kitchener Memorial Auditorium, honoured by this outstanding junior franchise.

CHAPTER 5

Caught in a Draft

"I never knew much about the draft, so I went to Montreal after the 1971 season. When I heard them say, 'The Montreal Canadiens pick Larry Robinson,' my mouth dropped to my knees." – LARRY ROBINSON (in *Hockey's 100* by Stan Fischler)

During my season with the Kitchener Rangers, there had been whispers about NHL scouts watching my progress. The *Kitchener Waterloo Record* reported, "Last weekend, Robinson's tidy defensive play had a couple of professional scouts waxing their palms. One of them said that Robinson may surprise a lot of people in the ranking of amateur draft selections in June [1971]. Robinson doesn't appear like he's accomplishing much with his loosey-goosey style. He's deceptive, though, [and] a lot of forwards have trouble beating him and offensively, he can bring that puck out when the heat's on."

There was no doubt who the first two picks were going to be at that year's NHL Amateur Draft. They were both guys I'd played against. Everyone was debating which one would be chosen by the Montreal Canadiens, who had the first pick. The Canadiens were about to announce that Jean Béliveau was retiring, and it was hoped that this pick might emerge as a successor to the legendary captain. Would it be Guy Lafleur or Marcel Dionne?

Lafleur had been sensational in the Quebec Major Junior Hockey League, leading it in scoring with 130 goals and 209 points for the Quebec Remparts. And Dionne had been almost as effective, playing fewer games but still leading the Ontario Hockey Association in scoring with 143 points, including 62 goals, for the St. Catharines Black Hawks.

Lafleur's Remparts and Dionne's Hawks were both champions of their respective leagues, and had met in the Eastern Canadian championship, with the winner to receive the George Richardson Memorial Trophy and a berth in the Memorial Cup final.

With the Remparts up three games to one, the fifth game was played at Maple Leaf Gardens in Toronto, with St. Catharines winning. It was a violent series, so much so that the Hawks then refused to return to Quebec City, where they had been spat on and had debris thrown at them on the ice. The Black Hawks offered to play the games elsewhere but were refused—so the team voted to forfeit the series, and the Richardson Trophy went to the Remparts.

Before the Memorial Cup championship, there was heated disagreement over player eligibility and travel subsidies that almost derailed the series—but the leagues ultimately agreed on a best-of-three set, with all games to be played in Quebec City. The Remparts would host the Edmonton Oil Kings, the champions of Western Canada.

It was a short one. With Lafleur starring, the Remparts won the first two games to claim the Memorial Cup, and popular thinking was that the Canadiens would select Guy with the first-overall pick.

I thought I had a pretty good chance of being picked myself, so after talking it over with my dad, we decided to make the two-hour drive to Montreal for the draft with Irwin and Evelyn Duncan.

We had gone to Expo 67 and La Ronde as our family vacation in 1967, and I thought the city was huge—it was the biggest city, by far, that I'd ever seen. Then we played the Montreal Jr. Canadiens in the OHA when I was with Kitchener, but truthfully, we never saw much of the city. We took the bus in, played the game, and took the bus back right after the game. The 1971 draft was only the third time I had ever been to Montreal.

We weren't used to big-city traffic and one-way streets, and didn't arrive at the Queen Elizabeth Hotel in downtown Montreal (where the draft was being held) until midway through the first round. We found a couple of seats in the big hall and watched intently as teams picked teenaged players. I didn't know what to expect, how it worked, or anything else. But I did find it kind of funny because, coming from the farm, it reminded us of a cattle auction. You go to the highest bidder.

I asked some of the guys sitting near us who had gone first, and as I suspected, Lafleur was the first player chosen and Dionne was the second pick (by the Detroit Red Wings).

I didn't know a lot of the guys getting picked later, but every once in a while, there'd be guys I had played against with the Rangers. I knew Steve Vickers and Steve Durbano from the Toronto Marlboros, and Terry O'Reilly was a tough winger with the Oshawa Generals.

The second round started, and while I didn't want to get my hopes up, with each selection, you *do* half hope that you'll hear your name. But then, when it finally happened, I wasn't expecting it. NHL president Clarence Campbell invited Montreal's general manager, Sam Pollock, to make the next selection—number 20—which was already Montreal's fourth of the day. "The Montreal Canadiens select Larry Robinson from the Kitchener Rangers."

I was stunned. You never fully believe that you heard your name called. I certainly didn't expect to go that high (though even if I had been picked number 50, I would have given it a shot). I also didn't expect to be picked by the Canadiens. In fact, I thought that if I went at all, I'd go to one of the expansion teams out west, because the only scout I had ever talked to was from the Los Angeles Kings. I knew that Claude Ruel had been to a lot of the junior games because he was renowned for being a great, great scout for Montreal. When you heard he was in town, you figured he was probably there to watch Dionne or some other player. I just never read anything into Claude being at any of the games Kitchener played.

I don't even remember who it was—it might have been Claude, but I'm not sure—that came over and congratulated me. He took me to meet Sam Pollock, Al MacNeil, and the rest of the Canadiens management. I shook so many hands that it's a blur today.

Before I was selected, the Canadiens had taken Chuck Arnason from the Flin Flon Bombers with the seventh pick and Murray Wilson from the Ottawa 67's with pick number 11. I was also pleased to hear that my friend, Teddy Scharf, who had played with me in Kitchener, was drafted by the Philadelphia Flyers. Though the expansion teams like Philadelphia were just starting to come into their own by 1971, the "Original Six" teams preyed on these weaker franchises by trading veteran players for their draft picks. Sam Pollock was a master at stockpiling draft picks for players who no longer fit into his plans with the Canadiens.

Oakland was a favoured trading partner for Pollock. In 1968, Montreal sent Norm Ferguson and future considerations to the Seals for Wally Boyer and Oakland's first-round picks in 1968 and 1970, *plus* future considerations. In June 1968, Montreal gave Oakland the opportunity to select Carol Vadnais in the 1969 waiver draft, and received their first- and third-round picks in the 1973 draft. Then, in May 1970, Sam sent Ernie Hicke and the Canadiens' first-round pick in 1970 to the Seals for their first-round pick in 1971 as well as a prospect and cash.

Clarence Campbell, the league president, said, "If we're ever going to get parity in the National Hockey League, some embargo must be placed on the trading of amateur draft choices."

In January 1971, Sam traded Ralph Backstrom to Los Angeles for two minor-leaguers and a second-round draft pick in 1973. It seemed like a fairly minor deal at the time, except Backstrom helped the Kings reach a playoff berth, pushing Oakland to a last-place finish. With the draft going in reverse order of where teams finished, that meant that Montreal got the first-overall pick in the draft—the pick they had received from Oakland for Ernie Hicke, which they used to select Guy Lafleur.

Sam looked like a genius, of course, but stated, "It was pure luck the way things turned out."

I always thought that my pick was owned by the Canadiens all along, but I was quite surprised to find out recently that, in fact, it was obtained in a trade with Los Angeles. It's a bit complex, so stay with me. During the summer of 1969, Montreal traded its first-round pick in 1969 (which turned out to be Dick Redmond) to the Minnesota North Stars for the promise that Minnesota wouldn't draft Dick Duff in the 1969 intra-league draft. Then, in January 1970, Sam sent Duff to L.A. and got Dennis Hextall and the Kings' second-round pick in 1971, and that pick turned out to be me!

Sam Pollock was so far ahead of everybody else, and was a very intimidating man, to say the least. Although, to be honest, all of these guys were intimidating to me. I was a small-town farm boy, after all.

I watched with interest how the hockey world was changing during the summer of 1972. The World Hockey Association emerged as a rival to the NHL, and a number of top names defected to the new league, which was offering huge salaries to attract marquee players such as Bernie Parent, Bobby Hull, and Derek Sanderson. I was drafted by the WHA, too—selected by the Ottawa Nationals. That was great, but my dream was to play in the NHL, and I watched closely to see how the Canadiens would be affected. The first player from Montreal to defect to the new league was Larry Pleau, my teammate with the Canadiens' farm team, the Nova Scotia Voyageurs, who signed with the New England Whalers. But of greater interest to me was that J.C. Tremblay, a veteran defenceman, left for the Quebec Nordiques after 13 seasons with Montreal. Perhaps this would open a spot for me.

CHAPTER 6

A Winning Welcome

"When Larry arrived, he gave our team a whole new dimension. He had the size, the shot, the skating, the ability, and he was easy to manage. He was good for the team in every way. You could say Larry was a dream player." – SERGE SAVARD

Claude Ruel contacted me a couple of weeks after the draft. He wanted to meet me at home in Metcalfe and discuss my first professional contract. Agents were a relatively recent phenomenon, and I had never even thought about securing someone to help me negotiate a contract. I wish my father had been there to help me, but he was away, so I was on my own.

Claude arrived at our home, and I introduced him to Jeannette, who had taken the day off work to support me. He explained that I'd likely spend a couple of seasons with the Nova Scotia Voyageurs of the American Hockey League before I got a shot with the Canadiens. He offered me $6,000 a year and a $6,500 bonus, with the promise that the amount would increase substantially when I was called up to the NHL. I was ready to sign, thinking to myself that this was $12,500—and I didn't even have $1,250 to my name at that point—but before I even had a chance to say anything, Claude increased the amount to $7,500 a year plus a signing bonus of $7,000. It was more money than I'd ever had. I was very pleased with the contract.

We invited Claude to stay for dinner, but he had to be on his way, so Jeannette and I celebrated with pork chops, my favourite meal.

•

Scotty Bowman had been brought in to replace Al MacNeil as coach of the Canadiens in 1971–72, which was a curious move; Al had been a rookie coach, but he'd guided the Canadiens to a Stanley Cup championship in 1971. But Al was English, and there was a French–English controversy within the Canadiens at the time. Al got into it with Henri Richard, and after his one season, he was replaced by Scotty, who was from Montreal and bilingual. Al was assigned the head coaching role with the Voyageurs.

To get myself ready for training camp, I did my usual football training, which I'd been doing through junior: wind sprints, push-ups, leg lifts, and things like that. I didn't know anything about work-out routines. I had never lifted weights, although from working on the farm, we were lifting big bales of hay, so I guess that was pretty comparable. By the time I was ready to leave for training camp, all I needed was to get back on skates. Back then, training camp lasted 28 days, so guys used that time to get in shape. We did two-a-day workouts and didn't even play an exhibition game until close to the start of the regular season.

Training camp that fall of 1971 was held in Montreal, at the Forum. I was handed some equipment in the dressing room, and the shin pads were way too short. There was a gap of four or five inches between the bottom of the pad and my foot. I'm almost six foot four and they were made for a much shorter player. When I turned the pads over and saw the number 9 written inside, I realized who the shorter player was: the Rocket, Maurice Richard! I wouldn't have said anything, but Guy Lapointe saw my predicament and brought Eddie Palchak, the equipment manager, over. "Eddie! What are you trying to do to the guy? He's going to break his ankles! Get the kid another pair of shin pads, for Christ's sake!"

The Canadiens had been pushed around a fair bit recently by teams like Boston's Big Bad Bruins and Philadelphia's Broad Street Bullies (a nickname that would be coined during my second pro season, but they were already consistently among the most penalized teams in the league). I was aware that Montreal wanted to add some size to the lineup, so when I was on the ice, I wasn't afraid to throw my weight around. During our first scrimmage, I ran Claude Larose, who was a veteran. He looked at me, stunned, and warned me that rookies weren't allowed to hit veterans. I didn't know that, but it didn't stop me.

In the dressing room, I sat in the corner and didn't say a word unless I was spoken to. I was just trying to learn the ropes. Guys like Guy Lapointe and Serge Savard really looked after me, almost like I was a brother, and that really helped me.

I had gone to camp just hoping to play well and find a place in the organization. I was disappointed, but not surprised, when I was sent to Halifax midway through training camp. I thought I hadn't made an impression on Montreal management. It wasn't until a few years later, when I was playing for the Canadiens, that Serge told me that the team had duly noted that I was a big guy who wasn't going to be pushed around.

I thought I would be stuck in the AHL for several years. After all, the Canadiens already had Pierre Bouchard, Terry Harper, Jacques

Laperriere, Guy Lapointe, Serge Savard, and J.C. Tremblay as regulars on defence—and at times, shifted Jimmy Roberts back to the blue line from his usual forward spot.

In Halifax, we had some good defencemen who, like me, were hoping for the call to Montreal. There was Murray Anderson, Bob Murdoch, and Bob Murray, and later, Noel Price and Dale Hoganson arrived, which added two more blueliners to Montreal's depth chart.

There were about 12 of us on the Voyageurs who lived in the same apartment complex in Dartmouth, including Anderson, Tony Featherstone, Mike Laughton, and their wives. Jeannette, Jeffery, and I had a little apartment there and got ourselves settled.

Kerry Ketter, a kid from B.C. who had also been sent to Halifax, got called up with me to play in an exhibition game against the Bruins. He was a defenceman, too, and we both wanted to impress Canadiens management. He and I were playing together, and lo and behold, Kerry whacks Johnny McKenzie. Next thing you know, the benches are emptying: here come the Big, Bad Bruins and, right behind them, the Canadiens. I'm playing in my first NHL exhibition game and here I am in a scrap. I can't remember who I fought, but by sticking up for your teammates, you earn your respect.

My coach with the Voyageurs, Al MacNeil, had been a very good NHL defenceman himself. I had heard stories about how he was one of the tougher guys in the league when he played for Chicago. And he was a tough customer as a coach. After playing a few exhibition contests, Al called me into his office. He sat me down and was very candid and stern with me. "Listen, young man. You're six-four and weigh 200 pounds. You're not using your size. If you're going to make it in the National Hockey League, you're going to have to play tougher. You're going to have to drop your gloves once in a while and get a little respect. Otherwise, you're not going to go anywhere. Unless you start playing tougher, we're going to have to send you to Muskegon."

I didn't know much about Muskegon, but I knew I sure didn't want to go there. It was in the International Hockey League, a level below the AHL and that much further away from the NHL. Plus I was a young guy with a family: I didn't want to move—and take the pay cut that would come with being demoted. The next game, I was in two fights and my career went ahead from there. I remember that there was a bench-clearing brawl in almost every game. The intimidation factor was huge back then, but that's how we learned the ropes.

MacNeil helped me develop into a defenceman who could play in the NHL. He was a great mentor to me. If he hadn't called me into his office and given me that talk, I probably would not have made it to Montreal.

Something else that really helped me was the trade in November 1971 that sent Rogie Vachon to Los Angeles. In return, the Canadiens got NHL veterans Dougie Robinson, Dale Hoganson, and Noel Price, who joined us in Halifax. Noel became my roommate on the road. He was a really good guy, and the Canadiens wanted Noel and his experience (he had first played in the NHL in 1957–58) to contribute to my growth. It was almost like I had my own instructor.

We had an older team, but we were solid. There were a few of us kids chomping at the bit to get to the NHL—Randy Rota, Murray Wilson, and myself—but our roster also had some guys who had already been to the show: guys like Mike Laughton, Noel Price, and Doug Robinson. There were also guys who had been toiling in the minors for several years, waiting for a break, including Rey Comeau, Germain Gagnon, and Kerry Ketter. Our goalies were Michel Plasse and Wayne Thomas. Wayne was one of the guys I used to hang around with, and he and I now work together in San Jose. Lynn Powis was another guy who was a good friend.

We learned as we went along, but the veteran presence really helped us young guys learn. We found out how to train and what it took to be a pro. MacNeil and Ruel worked with us every day, helping us with our skating and positional play. Al showed a great deal of confidence in me, using me in every situation—even-strength, killing penalties, on the power play. He played the crap out of me, and it really helped me develop. Al gave *The Hockey News* this assessment of me: "Larry's got a long reach, has great puck-carrying ability and is an excellent skater for a big man. He's plenty rough, or, at least as rough as he has to be. And he's smart. But he needs some polish to become an NHLer. He's got to work a bit on his defensive moves when guys are coming in on him, but he has no real weakness. He'll turn out to be a good one. He's got all the things he needs to become a National Hockey League star."

I didn't really spend much time thinking about playing in Montreal; I was enjoying my time with Halifax. I put on about 10 pounds and really learned to play with efficiency and toughness. We had a great team and finished second that season. Germain Gagnon led us in scoring, Chuck Arnason was our top goal scorer, and Ron Busniuk led the team in penalty minutes, but he could play.

We got on a roll in the playoffs. Michel Plasse was in goal and he got especially hot. We played the Boston Braves, the Bruins' farm club, who were drawing as many fans as the Bruins were at the old Garden. Those were great games. We eliminated Boston and went on to play the Baltimore Clippers for the Calder Cup championship. The series went to seven games, with the deciding game played at the Halifax Forum. Capacity there was something like 5,500, but they announced a crowd of 7,200 for game seven. They filled the place to the rafters. The Voyageurs won, and we were the very first Canadian team to win an AHL championship. The city had big parade through downtown Halifax for us. It was a great year, a memorable year!

After we won the championship, I hired two guys to look after my hockey affairs and was with them for three or four years, until they negotiated a deal with Sam Pollock without me even knowing. I was really pissed off about that and began discussing my career instead with Norm Caplan, a lawyer in Montreal who partnered with an agent in New York named Art Kaminsky. They handled a lot of players, including Guy Lafleur, and I decided to go with Norm. When I went to tell my previous representatives that I was changing agents, you should have heard the language! But I simply told them I was doing it, and that was that. Norm was terrific and took great care of me, including negotiations, all of my financial planning, taxes, everything. He was unbelievable.

Norm was a short, stocky guy, probably a hundred pounds overweight, and a workaholic. A bunch of us on his roster told him he had to slow down, that he was killing himself. He and his wife, Bella, decided to take a holiday to France in 1984, and they had just landed when Norm told Bella he wasn't feeling well and went to lie down. He had a massive heart attack. He was only 40 when he died. Such a nice man; it was a real tragic moment for us. I didn't have an agent after that.

I went back to the farm with Jeannette and Jeffery that summer, flying high after winning a championship in my first pro season. I got a job with the Ontario Department of Highways, helping build Highway 417 between Ottawa and Montreal. The stretch of highway they had me working on was between Russell and Maxville, so I was close to home. It was hot, tiring work, and they had us working 12-hour shifts each day, but it kept me in shape for training camp that fall.

Meanwhile, I'd always loved to play ball, and I joined Turpin Pontiac of the Ottawa Valley Fastball League. I was a long ball–hitting outfielder. I'll bet I played 50 or 60 ball games that summer. We had an incredible pitcher named Joe Belisle; he probably weighed all of 140 pounds, but this was a guy who could throw smoke. When he pitched, there was always the expectation that he'd deliver a no-hitter, he was that good.

When summer was over, I attended the Canadiens' training camp in September 1972, this time with a lot more confidence. I knew a lot of the guys, some from Nova Scotia and some of the veteran Canadiens I'd met at my first camp. That year was a little lighter than usual, since Yvan Cournoyer, Kenny Dryden, Guy Lapointe, Frank and Peter Mahovlich, and Serge Savard were all at Team Canada's training camp for the upcoming Summit Series. Alan Eagleson, one of the organizers, added three of his clients to fill out the roster for scrimmages: Billy Harris, John Van Boxmeer, and Michel Larocque. Both Van Boxmeer and goaltender Larocque were Montreal property.

With fewer players at training camp, I hoped I'd get a really good opportunity to be evaluated—and to make the big squad. With a year of pro hockey under my belt, I was better prepared when it came to what to expect. I knew they wanted me to use my size and be more aggressive, so during an exhibition game with Toronto, Pierre Jarry was whacking Jacques Lemaire, and I skated up to him and gave him a push and told him to watch himself. Jarry wasn't a tough guy, but you don't take liberties with our players. Surprisingly, he turned and dropped his gloves. I figured, "Okay, here we go," and punched him. Down he went. That was it. He bled like a stuck pig, and they carried him off the ice. My hand was a little swollen the next day.

But that was the kind of thing I quickly learned: in hockey, standing up for your teammates is the most important of the unwritten rules. I fought a lot of battles for my guys, but they fought a lot for me, too.

Even though I had spent a year in the minors, it turned out that my path to the NHL hadn't gotten any easier. The Canadiens were still deep in defencemen: they had Pierre Bouchard, Jacques Laperrière, Guy Lapointe, and Serge Savard locked in, plus guys like Dale Hoganson, Bob Murdoch, and Van Boxmeer, all with some NHL experience.

It looked like all the spots were taken, and would be for a while. But then something changed the landscape. The World Hockey Association emerged in 1972 as a rival to the National Hockey League. I hadn't heard anything about this rival league, and watched it from a distance with only modest interest. Although I was drafted by a franchise called the Ottawa Nationals, I had only one objective, and that was to play in the NHL.

The WHA had an impact on the club when J.C. Tremblay, one of Montreal's reliable veteran defencemen, jumped to the Quebec Nordiques (our future rivals). Along with the departure of Tremblay, Terry Harper was traded to the Los Angeles Kings. Suddenly, there were openings on the Montreal blue line.

I thought I had a really good camp in 1972. I was with the Canadiens at the home opener, which was against Minnesota, but I didn't play—I sat in the press box. And then, the next day, they sent me back to Halifax. It was a tough pill to swallow, but despite the losses of Tremblay and Harper, the Canadiens still had a wealth of defenceman and could afford to bring their young guys along slowly. It was the Montreal way. Yvan Cournoyer himself was almost exclusively a power-play specialist when the Canadiens first brought him up, and he didn't earn a regular spot for a few seasons. I was encouraged, though, when I was told the Canadiens would be keeping a close eye on me in Halifax. Scotty told me to keep my offensive game strong, but to work on the defensive elements of my game.

In mid-December 1972, I was invited to join the Montreal Junior Canadiens of the Quebec Major Junior Hockey League for an exhibition game against the Moscow Selects. Several of us from the Voyageurs were added to bolster the roster: Bunny Larocque was chosen in goal, but was injured and couldn't play, so they went with our backup, Michel Deguise. Dave Gardner, John Van Boxmeer, and I played as well. Midway through the second period, I stepped into a Soviet winger and knocked him cold. A hush fell over the crowd, and then a great ovation. It was a clean hit, but I was concerned that the player was badly injured. The game ended in a 3–3 tie.

After the exhibition, I had a brief Christmas with the family, but the best gift of all came early in the new year. The Voyageurs had just played a home game and a group of us were eating at a little restaurant right beside the arena. One of the guys came over and told me that Al wanted to see me. I got up from the table and went back into the Halifax Forum and knocked on Al's office door.

"Sit down, Larry," he said. "Montreal just called. Laperrière and Bouchard are out with injuries. They want you to join them."

I was stunned. "When?"

"Right away," he replied. "You'll leave tomorrow morning." Then he reminded me of the advice he had given me: "You've got to play physical, Larry. The best advice I can give you is to go out on your first shift, just look for somebody, and go out there and hammer them. That'll set the tone and let the Canadiens know that you're there to play."

Al shook my hand and wished me good luck. I went back into the restaurant and we had a couple of beers to celebrate.

Jeannette drove me to the airport and I flew to Montreal, took a taxi to the fabled arena at the corner of St. Catherine and Atwater, and reported for duty. Although I had spent time in the Forum during training camps, this time was entirely different.

I was given jersey number 19. For some reason, in Montreal it was a defenceman's number. Terry Harper had worn it before me, and before him, it was worn by Lou Fontinato, Junior Langlois, and

Dollard St. Laurent. But it wouldn't have mattered what number they gave me: it was the sweater of an NHL team, and that's all that counted to me.

I played my first game in the National Hockey League on January 8, 1973, at the Forum against the Minnesota North Stars. I was nervous, but I didn't come into the league with any fanfare, so that took away a lot of the pressure (other than the pressure I put on myself). On my first shift, I remembered what Al MacNeil had told me. The first player I had the chance to hit was Bob Nevin, an NHL veteran. I hammered him in the corner and knocked him on his ass. The crowd stood and cheered. That gave me a lot of confidence, and after that, the butterflies were gone and it became just another hockey game. Candidly, I don't remember anything about that game except that first hit. I had to look up details to find out that we ended up tying the game, 3–3.

In his excellent book *The Game,* Ken Dryden remembered that first game. "When I walked into the dressing room before the game, there he was, already half-dressed, looking taller, more rawboned, more angular than he does now. He played a remarkable game—poised, in solid control defensively, moving surprisingly well with only a hint of lanky awkwardness. And what I recall most vividly was that he blocked shots."

I never played another game in the minors.

Two weeks later, Scotty told me to find a place to live because I'd be staying with the Canadiens. I called Jeannette immediately and told her the great news. She packed our things, my dad and my sister-in-law met her and Jeffery in Halifax, and the four drove to Montreal.

The guys were very quick to welcome me. I had been around them for a couple of training camps, so that helped. And the young guys bonded pretty quickly, too. There were a few of us who spent a fair bit of time together: Bob Gainey, Guy Lafleur, Guy Lapointe,

Jacques Lemaire, Steve Shutt, Murray Wilson. I believe that that really contributed a great deal to our later success. We became just like family.

In those days, you noticed right away that the team was very close. I remember going to parties with Serge, Claude Larose, and all the guys. The only guy who almost never showed up was Kenny Dryden. Everybody else hung around together. I remember Yvan Cournoyer, who was a big star, coming to pick me up at my place. When we started out in Montreal, Jeannette and I rented a place on 48th Avenue in Lachine. We were next-door neighbours with Yvon Lambert and his wife, so Jeannette spent a lot of time with Sandy. Jeannette and Cathy Gainey, God rest her soul, became good friends as well, as did Murray Wilson and Steve Shutt's wives.

Early on, I played most of the time with Jacques Laperrière. He was a great veteran to be paired with—an excellent shot blocker and one of the best at playing a two-on-one. Lappy always seemed to get his stick on the puck. Off the ice, he was a real trickster, too. He had these little boxes, and if you opened one, this furry thing would jump out and scare you. He also had this crazy trumpet that he used for hunting. There was a trick to blowing it: you had to have really strong lungs and had to blow really hard to get a noise out of it. But he'd have put powder inside it, so if you blew really hard, the powder would fly out and right into your face. That's the kind of guy he was.

I didn't get a lot of points that first season, but I played fairly regularly and learned a lot. I scored my first NHL goal against Rogie Vachon in a 7–1 win over the Kings in Los Angeles on February 3, 1973. I actually didn't remember that, but when I went to L.A. in 1989, Rogie was the general manager, and he reminded me.

The Canadiens were dominant in 1972–73, finishing first overall. But even though I had played regularly through the season, when we started the playoffs against the Buffalo Sabres, I wasn't in the lineup; I was relegated to the Black Aces—the guys who weren't playing but were still on the roster. We got our asses skated off every day by Floyd Curry, who was assistant manager of the Canadiens at the time, and then we watched the games at night.

We beat the Sabres and moved on to play the Philadelphia Flyers, but Scotty only used me for one shift in Game One, and we lost that game when Rick MacLeish scored in overtime. I didn't really get much ice time until Laperrière got hurt in the third period of Game Two.

At the end of the period, we were tied 3–3, and Scotty threw me out onto the ice in overtime. Gary Dornhoefer had cleared the puck into our end. I picked up the puck behind our goal. I was going to pass it to Frank Mahovlich, but Frank yelled for me to keep going, and I took off down the left side. Just over the blue line, I fired a slapshot at the net—and it went over Doug Favell's glove hand for an overtime goal. I had only scored a couple of goals during the season, and for me, this was the ultimate high: my first time in the NHL playoffs and I scored an overtime goal that tied the series! I jumped around like a crazy fool and got mobbed by everybody. What a feeling that was! They named me the third star of the game and I got my first interview on national TV. I remember being extremely nervous, but very happy because I knew everybody back home was watching.

Montreal went on to win the next three games and eliminate the Flyers, which set us up for the Stanley Cup final against the Black Hawks, my team when I was growing up (but that had long faded into the past). The Hawks finished first in the West Division, so we were going to have a tough series. It was being billed as a battle of the goaltenders: Tony O (Esposito) against Kenny Dryden.

We quickly went up three games to one, and were all set to win it at home in Game Five. They had a big postgame party set up at the Queen Elizabeth Hotel. But we'd gotten ahead of ourselves, because then there was the famous 8–7 game that Chicago won. What a night! The first seven shots on goal went in: the shots on goals were four to three and so was the score. Just before Chicago's winning goal, I tried to hit Ralph Backstrom along the boards, but I missed him. I tried to get back as the Hawks went in and scored, but ended up inside the net behind Kenny after the puck went in. They threw everything they had at Kenny Dryden, and those 15 goals set an NHL record for most goals scored in a single playoff game. The loss meant that we had to go back to Chicago for Game Six, to try to clinch the Cup.

It didn't start off well. We were losing 2–0 with less than a minute left in the first period when Henri Richard scored to make it 2–1 and get us back into it. One thing I remember about Chicago Stadium was the stupid staircase you had to climb to get from your dressing room to the rink. We came out flying in the second period, and by the end of that 20 minutes, we were tied 4–4. We scored two more in the third and won the game—and the Stanley Cup—in Chicago.

I remember coming off the ice with Yvan Cournoyer and somebody threw a liquor bottle at us. It landed on the boards right beside us, and Yvan ended up getting cut from the flying glass. But the Chicago fans were normally pretty good, and it was really loud. When you were standing out on the ice and that organ was playing and the people were going crazy, Chicago Stadium could be a very special place. But it only takes one crazy fool to do something stupid like throwing a bottle to ruin it for everybody.

Claude Larose had broken his leg crashing into the post in the second period, and after the celebrations we went over to the hospital to pick him up to bring back on the plane to Montreal. When we arrived home, we had to carry him off the plane on a stretcher.

We received a $19,000 bonus for winning the Stanley Cup that spring. I used the money to buy my first gift to myself: a '73 Corvette Stingray. That was a great series, but I learned pretty quickly that when you're a Montreal Canadien, you are expected to win. The fans don't accept anything less. Still, the pride in playing for the Stanley Cup and getting your name engraved on it is what it's all about. That's something that can never be taken away from me.

CHAPTER 7

The Robinson Routine

"Playing in Montreal can do one of two things to a player: it can make you or break you. It made me. It brought out the best in me." – LARRY ROBINSON

Throughout my entire career, I pretty much had the same game-day routine. I'm an early riser, and on the day of a game, I liked to get up at about 7:30 a.m. The kids were usually up bright and early as well. I would have a good breakfast—usually cereal, juice, two eggs, bacon, toast, and a glass of milk.

On game days, we usually had an optional practice at 10:30. I didn't like to skate the morning of a game—if I felt bad, then I thought I'd take that into the game that night, and if I felt great, I was afraid I might be nonchalant in the game. So I usually took advantage of the option, which gave me the opportunity to watch Jeffery's hockey team play.

The rest of the time, our practices were very competitive. Back then, you had two scoring lines and two checking lines, so Scotty would have the Lemaire-Lafleur-Shutt line facing Bob Gainey's line. Even in practice, we were playing against the best players in the world! A lot of reporters and some of the players I played against would say that they loved to watch our practices because they were as good as the games we played. They were high tempo. If we were playing two or three games over a short period of time, Scotty would usually kick me, Serge Savard, and Guy Lapointe off the ice and tell the other three defenceman to keep working, whether it was Brian Engblom, Rod Langway, Pierre Bouchard, or whoever. The top guys who played a lot would practise less and less as the season wore on.

If I did attend an optional practice, I'd arrive at the Forum about an hour early, go for a light skate, and take a few shots. Nothing too strenuous. Some of the guys like to hang back after practice to work on their sticks and get their skates sharpened, but I liked to get changed quickly and get home. It was usually about a 30-minute drive.

The one thing I hated doing most was preparing my sticks. We used wooden sticks then, so out of a dozen, there might be four or five that would be just the way I liked them. Some arrived with too much of a curve, and others wouldn't be curved enough—so I'd have to heat them and make the curve a little bigger. I was always adjusting my sticks, whether it was shaving the heel, shaving the toe, or changing the lie. There were times when I'd lengthen the blade, while at other times I might take a quarter of an inch off.

When I first came into the league I used a much longer stick, but it was Jacques Laperrière, who was also a tall defenceman, who convinced me to use a shorter stick. I think I lost something off my shot by using a shorter shaft, but it felt more comfortable because, as a defenceman, you're so often working around the net with the puck at your feet. A shorter stick meant I had better control. Besides, I still had long arms, so I didn't lose that much of my reach. I wasn't particularly fussy about taping the blade of the stick, but I was always trying to get just the right size of the knob where it felt comfortable in my hand. That's what I tinkered with the most.

I didn't like really, really sharp skates. I like to glide on top of the ice, not dig into it. Unless I had a nick in my skate blade, getting my skates sharpened once a week would be a lot. Eddie Palchak, our trainer and equipment manager, was a special man. He was with the Canadiens for 31 years, and I went through my whole career in Montreal with him as a trainer. Eddie just knew my skates; he knew exactly how to sharpen them. He was one of the best.

I liked to eat early on game day as well. Between noon and one o'clock, I'd have a steak, mashed potatoes, vegetables, and some spaghetti. I never drank milk with my meal because it thickened the saliva and made it difficult to breathe during a game. Instead, I'd have a couple of ginger ales. That was the only time I ever drank soda. After lunch, I took a nap for an hour or so to relax. When I got up, I'd have a cup of coffee, put on my suit, and get ready to head to the rink.

Early on, I drove in with Pete Mahovlich, who lived nearby, but later, Mario Tremblay and I drove in together. I didn't like to get to the rink too early. We'd arrive just before our team meeting, by which time Guy Lafleur would already be dressed and have smoked three or four cigarettes.

Equipment was probably twice as heavy as it is today. The pants are so light today compared to what I wore in the '70s. I have long legs, but I didn't like my shin pads to be too long (though, of course, the Rocket's were too short!). I didn't like the bottom of the shin pad to reach my ankles because when you flex your ankles a lot, it would give you lace-bite.

We would wear our sweaters, one for home and on for away, from the first exhibition game of the season right through until the playoffs. Then, when playoff time came, Eddie would bring out new sweaters for us and we'd wear those until the season was over.

And those same sweaters would be the ones we'd wear to start the following season.

An hour before we took our pre-game skate, the coaches went over details with the team, and we'd talk about our approach to the game. That's when I really started to psych myself up. I really studied the opposing team, and our coaches prepared us well. I liked to know who had been hot for the other team, which goalie was starting, and who was injured on their team.

Different players have different ways of preparing for a game. Ken Dryden was always very quiet. He really spent time with his own thoughts. Lafleur and Shutt were quiet, too. Doug Risebrough was the opposite. He chattered all the time to get himself prepared. Pointu—as we called Guy Lapointe—joked around while he was getting ready. Bob Gainey used to go to each player's stall and talk to each of the guys. But as the game was nearing, the dressing room usually fell silent. Everyone was concentrating on the game.

We weren't an especially superstitious group, but we did have our routines. Before I'd step out onto the ice, Eddie Palchak would come over and use a polishing stone—we called it the "magic stone"—on each one of my skates, then give me two taps on each foot. We always followed Flower out onto the ice, gave him a couple of taps and then a whack in the rear end, and that was it. Later on, Craig Ludwig would stay by the net and make sure he was the last one to leave the ice before a game. All of us would tap everybody and then tap him. He'd wait until everybody else was gone, and then he'd whack the goalie's pads and be the last one away from the net.

I loved to chew gum while I was playing. It relaxed me out there. Between periods, most of us loosened our skates to get the blood in our feet circulating. I perspired so much that I would take off my sweater and my shoulder and elbow pads and change my undershirt. It was the old Stanfield underwear; you'd get so hot wearing it, and it soaked up all the sweat and then weighed a ton, so I'd feel a lot better once I did that. There was always Gatorade or sodas for guys, plus oranges. I'd always suck on some oranges and reflect on what had (and hadn't) happened. I relived plays, usually mistakes, in my head. The coaches usually didn't say a lot between periods. They might remind us of something, but it was never a rah-rah pep talk. As we were filing out of the room to start the new period, it might be something like "C'mon guys! Let's get one quick!"

When the game was over, win or lose, the dressing room was noisy. Guys were talking about the game amongst themselves, but there was also usually a roomful of reporters looking for quotes to meet their deadline. They'd naturally try to isolate one of the stars of the game and ask about a play. We all appreciated that it was part of the job and were accommodating and courteous, even when we didn't really feel like talking, specifically after a loss.

Arriving early, Guy Lafleur was also unbelievably quick to leave after a game. He'd shower, dress, and be gone while most of us were still taking off our equipment. I was notoriously slow. I liked to take my time. The trainers used to kid me, "Hey Robby, be sure to turn off the lights and lock the door when you leave!"

After a game, Jeannette and I would go for dinner, usually with a few other players and their wives. Traditionally, we ate at a restaurant on the West Island, not far from home. We'd be hungry because we hadn't eaten since noon. I'd have a couple of beers to replace the fluids I lost during the game (I used to lose as much as six or seven pounds). It was never a rowdy evening. Good conversation amongst friends.

It would take me an hour or two to unwind after getting home, although I'd be tired, and once I hit the pillow I was gone for the night. Hockey is a very demanding, high-energy profession with intense scheduling, so I knew the importance of getting a good rest.

And then, next game day, we'd start all over again.

CHAPTER 8

On the Verge of Success

"Gradually, his choppy, legs-akimbo stride lengthened and grew forceful; the dangerously erratic shots that had sent teammates from the front of the net to the relative safety of the corners now came in low enough often enough to bring them back for rebounds; his puck-handling and passing more confident and certain. [Robinson] was becoming an immense ragbag of rapidly developing skills." – KEN DRYDEN (in *The Game*)

It was beyond a dream that, in my first partial NHL season, we won the Stanley Cup. My goal for 1973–74 was to earn a full-time position on the Montreal Canadiens' defence, and to my great relief and delight, I not only played regularly with the club for the next many years, but I was fortunate enough to become a key member of a team that went on to enjoy unprecedented success.

There were so many reasons why the team was so successful, but at the core was Sam Pollock. Sam had been part of the Canadiens organization since the mid-1940s. He learned the game at the feet of Frank Selke, who had masterminded the Canadiens through the 1950s and the run of five consecutive Stanley Cup championships the franchise won in the latter half of the decade. When Selke retired after the 1963–64 season, Pollock was hired as the general manager. Even though he was replacing a legend, Sam was incredibly shrewd and had extraordinary vision for the Canadiens.

Sam's fingerprints were all over the Stanley Cup–winning teams. Jean Béliveau said that Sam was "perhaps the finest hockey man who ever existed, and I say that knowing that Frank Selke preceded him. I admired not only his superb hockey knowledge, but also his tremendous ability to shoulder a killing workload. When people ask how the Canadiens could be so good over such a long period of time, two answers come immediately to mind: Frank Selke and Sam Pollock."

I had always heard how hard Sam worked, and longtime referee Red Storey confirmed it. "Sam had a tremendous asset that put him far ahead of his opposition. He was very, very dedicated and worked 18 to 20 hours a day while the other managers were working eight to 10. He not only worked harder, he was smarter, and a guy who can put those two things together is going to be more successful."

Sam put together the teams that enjoyed so much success in the 1970s, but remember that the Canadiens won the Stanley Cup four times in the 1960s, too (1965, 1966, 1968, and 1969), largely because of Sam. As another Red, journalist Red Fisher, told author T.C. Denault: "His need to win was more important than anything else. Nothing else mattered. Was Sam Pollock smarter than any of his peers? Probably. Did he work harder at his job? Definitely!"

In constructing the team that was so successful in the 1970s, Sam made a few trades that showed great vision. One of his first was deemed a very minor deal at the time, but it proved to be one of the most important in Montreal's hockey history. Sam sent Guy Allen and Paul Reid to Boston in 1964 for Alex Campbell and a goalie named Ken Dryden. None of the others played a single NHL game, but Kenny was one of the key members of the Canadiens during the 1970s and won the Conn Smythe Trophy in 1971 after playing just a handful of regular-season games in his first season.

As mentioned, Sam was also a wizard at stockpiling draft picks. In 1968, Sam sent Gerry Desjardins, a goalie prospect, to the Kings and received first-round draft picks in 1969 and 1972. That 1972 pick brought Steve Shutt to the Canadiens. In 1973, he traded Bob Murdoch and Randy Rota to Los Angeles for the Kings' first-round selection in 1974 plus cash. He used the draft pick to select Mario Tremblay. That same year, Dave Gardner was sent to St. Louis for the Blues' first-round pick, with which he chose Doug Risebrough.

From 1969 to 1974, Montreal had accumulated 17 first-round draft picks and eight second-round picks. In 1972, the Canadiens had four of the draft's first 14 picks, and in 1974, we held five of the first 15. Some of the players selected included Bob Gainey, Réjean Houle, Guy Lafleur, Michel Larocque, Marc Tardif, and Murray Wilson. "I get a little upset with people when they tell me how lucky we are to have great players like Lafleur, Lapointe, Savard, and Robinson," Sam said. "We scouted them; we assessed them. That's not luck . . . that's hard work!"

Sam seamlessly worked new stars into the lineup to replace aging or retiring veterans, so that the rebuilding of the franchise was done simultaneously with the changing of the guard—a blueprint followed by the most successful teams in other sports. There was no period of readjustment as stars like Jean Béliveau, Henri Richard, and Gump Worsley left and prodigies like Guy Lapointe, Jacques Lemaire, and Serge Savard (as well as the players above) were introduced onto the roster. One of Sam's boldest moves, again, was installing Scotty Bowman as coach of the Canadiens to replace Al

MacNeil in 1971 after Al had just led the Canadiens to the Stanley Cup. As much as I liked Al and appreciated what he did for me personally, it turned out to be a genius strategic move by Sam for the Canadiens.

In *Lions in Winter* by Chrys Goyens and Allan Turowetz, Sam explained how he built the team that was so successful in the 1970s. "You build a top-notch organization manned by the best people at all levels. You get each man doing his job on the ice and off the ice and all of a sudden, you're a winner. Believe it or not, that's the easy part. Where most sports organizations go wrong is in letting up once they have reached, or are near, the top of their sport. Once you're a winner, you keep improving on perfection. You keep making trades and changes that will strengthen their team. That is where we might have been different from other franchises. Once we started winning, we worked even harder to continue winning, too many organizations relax at this point."

•

But the 1970s weren't without problems. After we won the Stanley Cup in 1973, we were feeling very good about the team's prospects at repeating in 1973–74. But then Kenny Dryden got into a salary dispute with Sam Pollock and walked away from the team. He had a contract that ran until the end of that season, but after backstopping the Canadiens to the Stanley Cup, he wanted to renegotiate. Ironically, he retired in order to article for a Toronto law firm at something like $7,500 for the year.

Pollock fumed, but it didn't change anything. Without Dryden, his backup, Wayne Thomas, assumed the role as our primary goaltender (although Scotty also used Michel Larocque and Michel Plasse at various times). Bunny Larocque was our goalie all through the playoffs that year. Dryden's retirement was quite a blow for us, but Kenny always marched to the beat of his own drummer and simply decided that hockey wasn't the only thing in his life. We had another strong season in his absence, finishing second in our division, but we lost to the Rangers in the opening round of the 1974 playoffs.

It's always an honour to be chosen to play in the All-Star Game, as I was in Chicago during January of 1974. Okay, I wasn't the first choice—that was Bobby Orr. But when Bobby was unable to play, they named Serge Savard to replace him. Then Serge was injured, so they picked Carol Vadnais, but Vadnais's coach wouldn't let him play, so I got selected. I was the replacement for the replacement for the replacement. Two years later in Philadelphia, I was only the replacement. That was progress, at least. In any case, it was still an honour to play!

•

Pollock and Dryden would ultimately agree to a new contract and Kenny was back in the fold with the Canadiens in 1974–75, but we lost a few other key players. Frank Mahovlich left to join the Toronto Toros in the WHA, and another loss that saddened me a great deal was the retirement of Jacques Laperrière. Furthermore, our captain, Henri Richard, broke his ankle early in the season and didn't return to the team until the spring.

We still had a great season, finishing first in our division and tied for first overall with Buffalo and Philadelphia. Ten of our guys scored 20 or more goals, including Serge and Lapointe from their blueline positions. And then there was Guy Lafleur, who enjoyed the breakout season we knew he was capable of. He scored 53 goals to break Montreal's regular-season goal-scoring record of 50 set by Maurice Richard and tied by Bernie "Boom Boom" Geoffrion.

We went a little further in the playoffs, beating Vancouver in the opening series, but were eliminated in the semifinals by Gilbert Perreault and the Buffalo Sabres, who in turn were crushed by the Flyers, who won their second straight Stanley Cup.

It was starting to look like the Flyers could simply bully their way to the Cup . . . but we would have something to say about that.

CHAPTER 9

Bringing Down the Hammer

"He was physically dominant. When the Canadiens went into Philly, he would take care of business. He could do everything."
– DOUG WILSON (in *The Hockey News Top 10: Counting Down the Game's Wonderful, Wild, Weird and Wacky!*)

We hated the Philadelphia Flyers. They were cocky assholes. In fact, I think almost every other team in the NHL hated the Flyers. The problem was, they were successful. Let me try to explain the Flyers.

They were called the Broad Street Bullies, and with good reason: they ruled through fear. While they had brilliant goalkeeping from Bernie Parent, and certainly had skill in front of the net, the biggest tool in their arsenal was intimidation, which they used abundantly to win hockey games. In most great dramas, you need heroes and villains, and the Flyers were both.

Their roster included guys who were quick to run you, stick you, or drop their gloves—whatever it took to earn a win. They had guys with names like Mad Dog Kelly, Moose Dupont, and, most notoriously, Dave "The Hammer" Schultz. In 1974–75, Schultz set an NHL record with 472 minutes in penalties! He was almost Lady Byng material the next season when he cut his penalty minutes down to 307. And then there were guys like Bobby Clarke, Gary Dornhoefer, Andre Dupont, and Bob Kelly, who regularly posted 100 or more minutes in penalties themselves. Don Saleski. Ed Van Impe. Orest Kindrachuk. Jack McIlhargey. These were tough boys, and the Flyers were detested around the league. I'd hear stories about guys coming down with the "Flyer flu" because they didn't want to play against Philadelphia.

One of their stars was Bill Barber, with whom I'd played in junior. Bill and I were pretty close when we played in Kitchener, and he and his wife, Jenny (who sadly has since passed away), used to hang out with Jeannette and me. When he went to Philadelphia, however, Bill became my enemy on the ice. To be fair, I didn't think of him the same way I thought of a lot of the other Flyers, and I even played with him on a couple of Canada Cup teams. He was an excellent player and had a great career.

There was a long history of hatred between our two teams. We were both successful teams, but we employed dramatically different styles to win contests. Our rivalry with the Flyers went back a long way, but I can pick out a few incidents that just put us over the top.

NBC used to televise games on Sunday afternoons, and on February 17, 1974, the network was scheduled to broadcast our game against the Flyers.

Early in the game, there was a delayed tripping call on John Van Boxmeer, but Dave Schultz decided to mete out his own sentence and cold-cocked Van Boxmeer with a single punch when he wasn't looking. Schultz was that kind of player. John never saw it coming and was left prone on the ice—out cold. Mad Dog Kelly boasted, "I've seen Schultzie throw some good ones, but never one like that."

Near the end of the period, I got clipped by a high stick myself, and because there were only seconds left, I went to the dressing room and started to take my skates off. The next thing I know, one of the ushers rushed into the room and yelled, "The benches have cleared!" As the period ended, Pierre Bouchard had slammed Flyer captain Bobby Clarke into the boards in the corner, which set off fireworks. The Flyers didn't let you touch their captain, and they stampeded off their bench. When our guys saw that, over the boards they went and everybody, goalies included, paired off.

I ran back out, stopping briefly at the bench to tighten the skate I had started to take off, and jumped back on the ice. I started to venture into the crowd of players, and out of the corner of my eye I saw Schultz heading towards Lafleur because they were the only two who hadn't partnered up in the scrum. I didn't grab Schultz in order to start a fight—I just didn't want him to go at Lafleur. We wrestled a little back and forth, pulling on each other's sweater. Then, he gave me a bit of a tug. I tugged back, and then he tried to butt me with his head. I was able to get my right hand loose and I started swinging. I got a couple of really good licks in. Schultz lost his balance and went down, and the next thing I know, guys were jumping on my back.

Art Skov, the referee, tried to keep track of all the infractions while the linesmen attempted to break up the worst of the scuffles. The problem was, every time they'd separate two combatants, another fight would break out elsewhere on the ice. Photographers streamed onto the ice to get shots of the melee, and finally, some police officers slid out onto the ice—not to break up the hockey fights but to usher the photographers off the ice.

When the mayhem was finally calmed, Skov handed out 91 minutes in penalties. Dupont and Kelly both got tossed for being the third man in, with Kelly getting an extra four for being the first one to leave the bench. Schultz and I got fighting majors, as did Bouchard and Clarke. Neither of them had actually thrown a punch, but it was their tussle that started the entire thing. Serge got two minutes and got tossed out of the game for leaving the penalty box. He had been serving his own five-minute major for high sticking when the fights broke out.

We were drained physically and emotionally after the fights, and although we had been up 2–0, the Flyers came back in the third and scored two to finish the game in a tie. But our fans stood and gave a tremendous ovation at the end of the game. It had been quite an evening!

"The Canadiens knew they had to play physically, and they matched us bump for bump," their coach, Fred Shero, said after the game. "The fight inspired us. Maybe they thought they had us, but you still have to hit, and I don't think they hit anyone in the third period."

I had been in tougher fights, but because I'd stood up to Schultz, considered the most feared fighter in the league at the time, I gained notoriety from that point on. I had embarrassed Schultz, and seldom had to fight from that point on. I became "the guy who beat up Dave 'The Hammer' Schultz."

In a November 1995 *Toronto Sun* article titled "Robinson's Fists Forged Canadiens' Dynasty," Al Strachan wrote, "The aspect of Larry Robinson's career that most often is overlooked is the fact that, in his time, he was the best fighter in the National Hockey League." While I'm not certain how true that was, my size certainly gave me some advantages, and those years of baling hay gave me a natural strength that I brought to my game. I much preferred to serve as a peacemaker when the occasion demanded, but if I had to fight, I didn't back away from dropping the gloves.

"Larry, by that time, just had this reputation around the league," Dryden said. "The thinking was, 'You just don't mess with this guy, you have no idea how strong and tough this guy is, and you don't want to find out.'"

But the lasting effect of that brawl with Philadelphia was that, all of a sudden, the Flyers didn't look so invincible. Serge Savard said, "This is not only a victory for the Canadiens, it is a victory for hockey. I hope that this era of intimidation and violence that is hurting our national sport is coming to an end."

The Flyers, disappointingly to us, would still go on to beat Boston for the Stanley Cup in 1974 and repeat against Buffalo in 1975, but the battle wasn't over. The following year, we had a home-and-home preseason series with the Flyers on Saturday and Sunday, September 20 and 21. The Broad Street Bullies were coming off their second Stanley Cup victory and were as cocky as ever. Even though it was an exhibition game, they sent a veteran lineup to Montreal. Saturday night was feisty, with lots of chirping but few incidents. At one point, Schultz crosschecked Yvan Cournoyer in the back. Dougie Risebrough refused to let Schultz get away with that, and the two dropped the gloves and went at it.

The next night, in Philadelphia, Scotty had an appropriate lineup ready. He dressed Pierre Bouchard, Rick Chartraw, Glenn Goldup, and Sean Shanahan—all big, tough boys. It was important that we show the Flyers that we might have been a skill team, but we could play their game, too. If we could eliminate the Flyers' physical edge, our superior hockey skills would allow us to beat them.

The game was a gong show from the start. Schultz was in three fights—two with Chartraw and one with Goldup—before the first period was over. We were up 6–2 with less than two minutes to go when Kelly of the Flyers took a roughing penalty. Scotty had had enough, so he sent out a power-play unit, but this one was not intending to score, it was to settle a score. He sent me out to play centre, with Glenn Goldup and Sean Shanahan on the wings and Pierre Bouchard and Rick Chartraw back on defence. We were all over six feet and 200 pounds, and Scotty was making a very clear statement to the Flyers: "We'll beat you with skill, we'll beat you with strength, we'll beat you anyway you want to play!"

The game had been decided, but it was a powder keg and any kind of spark would set the whole thing off. As Bobby Clarke and his line skated to the bench for a rest, the sparks ignited and things erupted. Risebrough and Clarke exchanged words, and then Dougie tackled Bobby. Schultz hurtled over the boards to get at Risebrough, followed by the rest of the Flyers. When we saw that, we leapt over the boards, too.

Everybody on both teams was involved in the brawl except Bernie Parent and Kenny Dryden, the two netminders (they stood off to the side and talked!). The main combatants really went at it. Ricky Chartraw, who had fought Schultz twice in the first period, went toe to toe with him again and beat him decisively. Glenn Goldup pummelled Jack McIlhargey, Lafleur got into it with Mel Bridgman, and then Mario Tremblay stepped in and finished that bout while Shanahan took on Gary Dornhoefer. Somehow or other, Clarke left the ice with that toothless grin, but also sporting a shiner.

Bruce Hood was the referee, and when he and the other officials had finally calmed the violence, he called the game off right then and there. A total of 332 minutes in penalties were assessed for that series of fights in the City of Brotherly Love, but something significant had taken place: we had shown that the Broad Street Bullies were not invincible. We showed that their brand of hockey could be contested. No longer were we—or other teams, for that matter—afraid to play the Philadelphia Flyers. We stood up to them, and, without our realizing it at the time, those games really pulled us together and taught us that we had all the ingredients needed to win.

With that brawl, the Philadelphia Flyers' reign of terror came to an end. In the book *Lions in Winter,* Steve Shutt beautifully summed up the importance of the incident: "We won the Stanley Cup that night. It just wasn't official until May."

CHAPTER 10

Emotional Rescue

"You couldn't help but get better because we had a bunch of guys who loved to be on the ice. Guy Lafleur loved to be on the ice. Steve Shutt loved to be on the ice. Larry Robinson loved to be on the ice and going at top speed. When we scrimmaged, you were playing against the best players in the world. It was fun!" – PETER MAHOVLICH (in *The Hockey News: Greatest Teams of All Time*)

When Henri Richard retired after the 1975–76 season, I had played with him for three seasons. "The Pocket Rocket" was a fierce competitor, and although only about five foot seven, he had a very mean streak in him. I had heard the stories even before I was with the Canadiens. Everybody assumed when little Henri came into the league, he was riding on the shirt-tails of his brother, because Maurice was a really tough customer, but I was told that, one night, Henri took on three of Boston's toughest guys, won the first two fights, and tied the third. Nobody had to worry about Henri after that. What epitomized the type of captain Henri Richard was? When we were down by a score of 2–0, who would get the big goal to get us back into the game? It was Henri. He wasn't a big goal scorer, but he scored big goals. He was a very heady, two-way hockey player who competed like a son of a gun. He didn't say a lot, so he was more of a captain who led by example, not unlike Bob Gainey. But when you've won the Stanley Cup 11 times in 20 seasons, you don't have to say a lot.

Henri was the last tie to the Canadiens dynasty of the 1950s, when Montreal won five consecutive Stanley Cup championships. But taking his place as captain was Yvan Cournoyer, who was himself part of the four Stanley Cup wins in five years in the 1960s.

I have never seen a team as involved emotionally as we were that year. We had a feeling amongst ourselves that the entire National Hockey League wanted us to win, just because of what the Flyers stood for. Principally because of what had taken place in that home-and-home preseason series with the Flyers, we were able to play our brand of firewagon hockey without being intimidated. We had an extraordinary season, setting an NHL record with 58 wins to go with 11 ties, while we lost only 11. After that, we had a relatively quick path to the Stanley Cup final. First, we swept Chicago and then took out the Islanders in five games. And wouldn't you know it? We met the Flyers for the Stanley Cup.

Philadelphia was the two-time defending Stanley Cup champion, but they almost didn't get their third shot at the Cup in 1976. They had a really tough series with Toronto, which went seven games before they finally won. After that, our matchup was highly anticipated.

"This series can be seen as a test of the kind of slick hockey that purists called 'traditional' against the currently popular rough-edged variety of play," said an article in the *New York Times*. "The teams both carry weighty reputations that will outlast their performances in one particular playoff series."

The games were all close, but that was the way we played. Our late-'70s team gets labelled as a skill team—and it was—but people forget how smothering our defence could be. We won the first game in Montreal by a single goal, and were leading 2–1 midway through the third period of Game Two when Dornhoefer started a rush up the right side. I angled towards him, and just inside our blue line, I got my hip into him and he hit the boards hard. This was that classic moment when he got up and we realized that we had broken the boards. We were also about to break the Flyers' championship streak. That hit seemed to take some of the wind out of their sails, and their belligerence largely disappeared.

Dornhoefer and I seemed to have an unspoken agreement that whenever the two of us met on the ice, there was going to be a collision. But there was actually no personal animosity. We were two competitors doing what we needed to do to help our teams win.

Game Three shifted to the Spectrum in Philadelphia. They had this tradition that whenever Kate Smith came out to sing "God Bless America," they rarely lost. The public address announcer introduced us first. We were all standing on the blue line, and people were going crazy: you could hardly hear anything. The next thing you know, they're starting to introduce their team. We just looked at each other, said, "To hell with this," and started skating around as they were being introduced. All of a sudden, you could feel the crowd starting to get quiet. We won that game, again by a single goal.

Knowing that, with one more win, the Stanley Cup was ours, we were more than ready for Game Four. It would be especially sweet to beat the Flyers, our enemies.

Usually, we warmed up about half an hour before the game was to start. We went out and did a few drills, got loosened up, and went back to the room. We couldn't wait. The only guy who wasn't walking around the room, pacing, was Kenny Dryden. He sat there, focused and deep in thought. I don't think anybody could have beaten us that night. We were that prepared and that hungry to beat them.

The Flyers, of course, once again brought out Kate Smith to sing "God Bless America," and introduced all their guys with spotlights. We just ignored the whole thing, mentally preparing ourselves for the game to start.

The game itself was, as usual, close, but there was no denying us. Flower's goal late in the third proved to be the Stanley Cup winner and we finished with a 5–3 victory. Yvan Cournoyer was handed the Cup by Clarence Campbell, and we whooped it up on the ice—never dreaming that we would do this again for the next three years. But to me, of all my Cups, that was the one that I cherish the most.

When we flew back from Philadelphia, we all went over to a restaurant on the North Shore owned by Claude St. Jean, who was a friend of Serge Savard's. He kept it open for us so we could celebrate, which we did until the wee hours of the morning. A security guard drove me home in my car because I couldn't drive—I couldn't even remember where I lived, so we drove up and down the street three or four times, hoping I'd recognize the house! At around four in the morning, Jeannette looked out, wondering where I was, and saw my car driving up and down the street, so she came out onto the road, waving. That's how I found my house that night!

The next day, we took the Stanley Cup to Crescent Street, and then to a bar that Henri Richard owned. Finally, on the third day, there was a victory parade. We rode down St. Catherine Street in convertibles. I had to laugh when the car carrying Murray Wilson died on him during the parade. It didn't seem to bother him—he stopped into a bar for a beer and caught up to the rest of us a little later.

It was during that Flyers series that I got tagged with the nickname Big Bird. The Flyers had a guy on their team named Don Saleski, and he had been called Big Bird because he somewhat resembled the Sesame Street character. In an interview, Serge said, "We've got our Big Bird, too. It's Larry Robinson." Back then, I had my hair permed. You have to remember the era, but after the game there were guys who would stand there blow-drying their hair, and then use hairspray. I just wanted something that I could towel-dry and then go, so the perm worked for me—well, at least for a while. So in Serge's mind, being tall and thin with permed hair made me resemble Big Bird.

And from there, it stuck. It's not something I'm enamoured of, but I can live with it or without it. I still get people who want me to sign pictures with my name and Big Bird.

CHAPTER 11

The Best Year of Our Lives

"I always felt that when you tell your guys what a great team the other team is, you weren't doing them any favours. If you did that with the Montreal Canadiens of the 1970s, you'd be beat before you even got started. 'Let's check their first line: Shutt with 60 goals, Lemaire with 34 goals, Lafleur with 56 goals.' Then you go to Robinson, Lapointe, Savard. You're saying how great they are. What's the sense of playing them?" – DON CHERRY (in *Don Cherry's Hockey Stories and Stuff*)

The 1976–77 season was incredible. "They were the most electrifying, dominant and unstoppable team the NHL has ever seen," said *The Hockey News*. We lost just eight games that season, winning 60 (breaking our own league mark) and tying 12. We also set an NHL record with 132 points. Ken Dryden said, "There were an inordinate number of games we won without a reasonable amount of difficulty." And we lost just once at home all season.

Guy Lafleur spoke for all of us when he said, "I will never accept losing. Never!" Yvan Cournoyer said, "It was one of those seasons where the less you lose, the more you want to win."

Flower won his second straight Art Ross Trophy as scoring leader as well as the Hart (most valuable player) and the Lester B. Pearson Award (most outstanding player, as selected by the players—it's now called the Ted Lindsay Award). I didn't keep track of my points at the time, but looking back, 1976–77 was a career best for me. I scored 19 goals and added 66 assists, and those 85 points set a team record for defencemen. Kenny Dryden and Michel Larocque were recipients of the Vézina Trophy for the best team goals-against average, Scotty was named coach of the year, and I was awarded the Norris Trophy as the best defenceman. Shutty was the league's top goal scorer, and if the Maurice Richard Trophy had existed then, he would have won that. Flower, Shutty, Kenny, and I were all named to the NHL's First All-Star Team, with Lapointe on the Second Team.

All year, Flower and Shutty got all the press—and they deserved it—but Jacques Lemaire was the key to the success of their line. And just a great guy, too.

We played St. Louis in the opening round of the playoffs. I remember it being so damned hot, and the hotel refused to turn on the air conditioning. I was rooming with Serge Savard, and we both took our mattresses out onto the balcony so we could at least be cool enough to fall asleep. We swept the Blues, thankfully, and couldn't get away from the Missouri heat fast enough.

Our semifinal series was against the Islanders, a really good, young team. They made us earn our wins. Bo—that's Bob Gainey—scored both goals for us in Game Six, a 2–1 victory that earned us a spot in the Stanley Cup final for a second consecutive season.

If the Flyers hoped to get revenge against us, however, their chances evaporated when Boston eliminated them in four straight games in their semifinal series. The Bruins were the team we had the toughest time with that season. That lone home loss we encountered was to them in October. Of the eight games we lost in that entire season, three of them were to the Bruins, and there we were, facing Boston in the Stanley Cup final.

We had an ongoing war with the Bruins, and these games were no different. In the second period of Game Two, Lafleur and Mike Milbury, who was a rookie that season, were sent off for slashing. In the third, Guy moved up the ice and fired the puck into their end so that we could make a change. Milbury went ballistic, claiming that Flower had deliberately shot the puck at his head. It turned into a war of words, and after the game Milbury called it "a third-class effort by a guy I now regard as a third-class person." Then he added, "I just wish I had taken his head off with that slash earlier. Too bad that I hadn't!" Looking ahead to Game Three, John Wensink snarled, "If I get on the ice, Lafleur will not come out alive." Flower just shrugged it off. While Milbury was given a misconduct near the end of the game for being the third man into a scrap between Pierre Bouchard and Terry O'Reilly, Guy answered by continuing to pile up points against the Bruins. We won the game 3–0 and Guy scored two of our goals.

I don't really think intimidation works in the playoffs. There's too much at stake. Winning in the playoffs really is simply hard work, and with that work, you earn your breaks.

The end of a remarkable season came in overtime in Game Four in Boston. We were up three games to none over the Bruins, with the score tied 1–1. The puck was in the corner, being pinned by a number of skates from both teams. The linesman hollered, "Keep it moving!" and one of the Bruins kicked the puck, but it went right to Flower. Guy quickly fired it towards the net, where Coco (Lemaire) was standing, unguarded, and he fired the puck past Cheevers to win the game—and the Stanley Cup.

Flower was the leading scorer in the playoffs with 26 points, including nine in our series against Boston, and was awarded the Conn Smythe Trophy.

Even Boston's Harry Sinden admitted that his Bruins had been outmatched: "They're the best team in hockey by a country mile."

As per usual, there was a Stanley Cup parade down St. Catherine Street for us, and after the parade concluded, we were escorted into the mayor's office, where we were to be greeted and congratulated by Mayor Jean Drapeau. As only Pete Mahovlich could (or would!) do, he took a seat behind the mayor's desk and casually put his feet up—his bare feet! We laughed so hard!

In the fall of 2013, *The Hockey News* published their "Greatest Teams of All-Time" issue, which placed the 1976–77 Montreal Canadiens at the very top of their list. "The 1976–77 Canadiens set the standard by which all other great teams in the NHL will continue to be measured." But I had to laugh when I read some of the press clippings from that era. After the Stanley Cup victory in 1977, I said, "I've had a very satisfying year. I did fairly well, but by no means did I do it all on my own. Look, I was raised on a farm—the only attention I ever got was from the animals. That big fellow over there [the Stanley Cup] is what's important to me."

It's true. Unless you hoist the Stanley Cup at the end of the season, it isn't truly a successful year. In Montreal, you were always in the spotlight. You couldn't let pressure distract you from your role. There were frustrations and annoyances, pressure and injuries, but when you win the Stanley Cup, it's worth all the aches and aggravation.

CHAPTER 12

Conn Man

"During the 1970s, [Larry Robinson] was the best D-man on arguably the best blueline of all time on the best team of all time." – KEN CAMPBELL (in *The Hockey News Top 10: Counting Down the Game's Wonderful, Wild, Weird and Wacky!*)

On August 4, 1977, Jeannette and I welcomed our second child, a beautiful daughter we named Rachelle. The baby was healthy and everything went well. Watching that birth was just the greatest thing that had ever happened to me.

We had had some tough times, medically, trying to have a second child. There had been two miscarriages in between the births of Jeffery and Rachelle. Finally, we decided to change doctors, and when we did, Jeannette carried the baby to term.

Jeannette was wearing a monitor for her contractions, and I was sitting there with her. She warned me that she didn't want to know when the next contraction was going to happen, but every time the monitor indicated an upcoming contraction, I would fidget and Jeannette could read me and would tense up. Finally, she kicked me out. "Get out of here, Larry. I told you I didn't want to know when they're coming!" Jeannette was in labour a long time—about 18 or 20 hours.

This new doctor, who was wonderful, stood six foot eleven. There was another couple in the hospital at the same time as Rachelle was being born, and that father was six foot eight. I'm six-four, and when I came out of the delivery room after cutting the umbilical cord, I was standing between the two of them and it was the first time in my life that I had to look up to the people I was talking to! It was an interesting off-season, to say the least.

After winning two straight Stanley Cup championships in dominant fashion, we had the same lineup returning for the 1977–78 season, so we were feeling pretty confident. But things can change so quickly. In November, Murray Wilson suffered a back injury and had a spinal fusion and missed the rest of the season. And Pointu was having another great season when a deflected shot caught him in the eye in December. He underwent delicate surgery, but recovered fully.

They were great teammates, but meanwhile Pete Mahovlich and I were the best of friends. He was a funny, funny guy. Back then, it was believed that big guys were slow and had poor hands. Well, Pete had to be six foot five, but believe me, he was a terrific stickhandler, great playmaker, and a very good skater. Pete was overshadowed by his brother, Frank, but they were entirely different guys, and Pete was consistently one of our best players.

We lived near each other and usually rode to and from the rink together. In fact, I rode in with him the night in late November 1977 when he got traded. He told me on the way to the rink that he had been dealt to Pittsburgh for Pierre Larouche. It broke my heart. I guess sooner or later we all learn about the business side of the game, but I never got used to it. I had been fortunate that the Canadiens roster had remained more or less intact until then, and the Mahovlich trade was really my first introduction to friends being traded. The next time I felt as deeply affected was in March of 1982, when Guy Lapointe was traded to St. Louis for a draft pick. I hated that part of the game. I still do.

We finished first once again in 1977–78, and the core of the team just kept getting stronger. Flower again led the league in points, with 132, including 60 goals, and was also awarded the Hart Trophy. The NHL had introduced a new annual award, the Frank J. Selke Trophy, for the best defensive forward, and the first recipient was Bob Gainey. Kenny and Bunny won the Vézina again, too. I don't want to appear nonchalant, because these were exceptional individual awards, won in some cases on repeated occasions, but for the Canadiens, it was about doing your job to the best of your ability so that the *team* could be successful.

Our first playoff opponents were the Detroit Red Wings, and we eliminated them in five games. Up next were the Toronto Maple Leafs. The Canadiens hadn't faced the Maple Leafs in a playoff series since the 1967 Stanley Cup final during Canada's Centennial year. Our 1978 series wasn't nearly as memorable, as we swept Toronto fairly readily. Their coach, Roger Neilson, just shrugged and admitted, "We lost to the best."

For the second straight spring, we faced the Boston Bruins in the Stanley Cup final. Don Cherry was coaching the Bruins, who had evolved from the offensively dominating team led by Bobby Orr and Phil Esposito in the early 1970s into what Don called the "Lunchpail Athletic Club." They ground you into the ground and hit like crazy, but they could still score: there were 11 guys on their team that season who scored 20 or more goals.

The media played up our rivalry, and our incredible offence, but their GM, Harry Sinden, tried to bring his guys back down to earth: "I kept telling our guys that it didn't matter how many 40-, 50- and 60-goal scorers the Canadiens had. It wasn't their offence that was their strongest point, it was their checking ability. They may have a bunch of superstars on that team, but they don't play like individuals. They're the best checking team in the National Hockey League and that's why they're so good."

The Bruins focused on trying to shut down Lafleur, but Flower still picked up a goal and two assists in the opening game of the series, a 4–1 win at the Forum. "When we're moving, I don't think there's anybody who can touch us," Guy told CBC Television after the game. Game Two was much closer: it took overtime for us to eke out a 3–2 win. In Boston for the third game, the Bruins scored in the first minute of play and went on to shut us out, 4–0.

The series, to that point, hadn't been particularly physical, but the fireworks really began in Game Four as Terry O'Reilly and I both picked up roughing penalties before the opening faceoff. In order to stir things up early in the game, Scotty sent out an intimidating line of Doug Risebrough at centre joined by four big blueliners: Pierre Bouchard on one wing and Serge on the other, with Gilles Lupien and me back on defence. When Don Cherry saw who we had on the ice, he countered by sending out Stan Jonathan at centre, with Terry O'Reilly and John Wensink on the wings. Oh boy . . .

Right off the faceoff deep in our zone, Lupien went after Wensink, but he wanted no part of a fight and the play continued. The play moved out to the blue line, where Jonathan threw a big hit on Serge. Lupien moved in and bumped Jonathan, and as the play was stopped for an offside, Bouchard stuck out his leg trying to dump Wensink. The Bruin ignored the action, but his teammate Stan Jonathan didn't. Even though he was much smaller than Bouchard, he challenged Pierre. The two went at it an epic scrap. Both guys landed flurries of punches, but then Jonathan switched hands and caught Pierre with a haymaker. Bouchard hit the ice hard, bleeding from what looked like a broken nose. In fact, I believe he also suffered a broken cheekbone.

That fight immediately precipitated another battle between Lupien and Wensink. Lupien was bloodied in the process, as was linesman Ray Scapinello. When things finally settled down, Wensink raised his arms in victory—which really pissed us off. Lupien went over to the Bruins' bench and challenged them to continue the fighting.

Although Scotty had issued the challenge by sending out his biggest boys, Boston had countered, and for a few minutes, it appeared that the Bruins were intent on running us out of their building. In the end, they beat us 4–3 in overtime to even the series.

But we stabilized things back in Montreal, pouring on the firepower. At one point, with the puck deep in our end, Serge left the puck for me behind our net. It was time to go. I skated up through centre and then cut to the right, went around Mike Milbury, and, after protecting the puck with my left leg, put it over Cheevers's shoulder. We were up 4–0 in the second before going on to take Game Five by a 4–1 score.

We finally finished off the Bruins in Game Six back in Boston, with Mario Tremblay playing the game of his life. He scored two goals as we ended the series with a 4–1 win to collect our third Stanley Cup in a row.

I shared the playoff scoring lead with Guy Lafleur, who finished the series bandaged about the head from a series of high sticks. We both collected 21 points, mine including 17 assists. I was very honoured to be chosen as the winner of the Conn Smythe Trophy as the most valuable player in that year's playoffs.

"Larry Robinson killed us single-handedly," Don Cherry remarked. "Nobody ever deserved the Conn Smythe Trophy more than that guy. There's nothing he can't do."

Coming from Grapes, that was a hell of a compliment.

CHAPTER 13

May the Fourth Be With You

"More than just an outstanding player, Robinson became a presence." – KEN DRYDEN (in *The Game*)

The 1978–79 season was a most interesting one. It began in August 1978, when Edward and Peter Bronfman, who had bought the Canadiens from the Molson family in 1971, sold the franchise to Molson Breweries. Sam Pollock, the architect of our third straight Stanley Cup championship—and his ninth in 14 years with the team—subsequently retired, having accomplished more than just about any executive in hockey's long history.

Our coach, Scotty Bowman, coveted the general manager's position vacated by Sam, but he was passed over and the Canadiens hired Irving Grundman. Scotty was definitely not pleased.

Elsewhere, after seven seasons, the World Hockey Association folded. A lot of positive things came out of the WHA: for us, it was specifically Rod Langway and Mark Napier joining the team.

Though he began the season with us, Yvan Cournoyer was having recurring back pain and finally had to call it a career in November. Replacing him as captain was my roommate and defence partner, Serge Savard.

Though we had dominated the NHL the previous three seasons and won the Stanley Cup in each of those years, in 1978–79 it was the New York Islanders who topped the standings at the end of the regular season (although they only beat us by a point). Candidly, we got a little complacent and lost to the Red Wings in the last game of the regular season, which cemented our second-place finish. Nevertheless, we finished first in our division.

Our offence was as potent as ever, led by Lafleur, who again scored more than 50 goals, and our defence was rock-solid. Our goaltenders won the Vézina for the fourth year in a row. Bob Gainey won the Selke for the second straight year, too.

But the Islanders had designs on the Stanley Cup every bit as much as we did. Like us a few years before, they had a talented, young team growing together and hungry to win. It wouldn't happen that year, as their archrivals, the New York Rangers, ended that dream for Long Island, eliminating them in the semifinals.

We faced Detroit in the first round of the postseason and sent them home in five games. Our series with the Maple Leafs was a lot tougher, although it turned out to be even shorter.

We badly outscored the Leafs in Games One and Two, but the games got much tighter from then on. It ended up taking us a couple of overtime wins to beat Toronto. The Leafs' goalie, Mike Palmateer, hurt his catching arm in the second game, so their backup, Paul Harrison, was in goal for Game Three. That one went to double overtime before Cam Connor scored to give us the win.

I scored early in the fourth game as we put up a commanding four-goal lead on the Leafs, but Toronto scored two goals 30 seconds apart in the third. We came unglued, and with the score tied at four and moments left in the game, Harrison made an unbelievable save on Lemaire to force overtime.

We were a couple of minutes into the extra period when Tiger Williams ran me and got called for high-sticking. Tiger could get a bit rambunctious, to say the least, but this was a marginal call at a really crucial time. He was furious, but became even more so when, on the ensuing power play, I fired a screened slapshot that Harrison never saw. It found the back of the net to win the game and the series. Tiger went ballistic! He roared out of the penalty box with one thing in mind—to hunt down referee Bob Myers. He later said, "I wanted to kill the son of a bitch."

Dan Maloney intercepted Tiger, tackling him so that he didn't do anything stupid. Several more of his teammates whipped over to try to settle Tiger down, but he wasn't hearing any of it.

I was celebrating the victory with my teammates when I looked over and saw what was going on. I skated over to Tiger and grabbed him and told him to forget it—that it was a horseshit call, but it was over and he shouldn't do anything stupid. I think I even told him I'd take him fishing that summer. It seemed to calm him right down. In his autobiography, he said, "Larry Robinson did me one of the biggest favours of my life. The big guy [me] saved my neck, because if I'd got hold of Myers, I'm sure I would have done him some serious damage."

Our path to a fourth Stanley Cup didn't get any easier, however. Our next opponents were, once again, the tough Boston Bruins. We had had some classic series in the Stanley Cup final with Boston, and this one was no different, although it was a semifinal matchup. We won the first two games at home, and then the Bruins took the next two in Boston. We again won at home, and then Boston won at home. The series was to be decided in a seventh game played at the Forum.

Boston knew that they had to contain Lafleur. And we knew that if we didn't go out and work our butts off, it was going to be an early summer for us, something we certainly weren't used to—and definitely weren't ready for.

Game Seven of that 1978–79 semifinal against Boston was the most physically demanding and emotional game I can remember playing. There had long been an intense rivalry between the two franchises. But we had beaten Boston in four straight in 1977 and in six games in 1978, and they wanted revenge.

Boston led 3–1 after two periods in Game Seven. We came back and scored two, the last on a power-play goal by Lapointe that Don Cherry disagreed with. Those of you who watch Don's "Coach's Corner" feature on *Hockey Night in Canada* have seen him bow with his arms raised as part of the opening: that was his sarcastic reaction to that power play. Meanwhile, only one shift after Pointu's tying goal, he was carried off the ice on a stretcher with a knee injury.

With four minutes left, Ricky Middleton scored to again put Boston ahead by a goal. It looked like we were done. But then the unimaginable happened. The Bruins took a penalty for having too many men on the ice! With three minutes left, I had passed the puck up to Mark Napier along the boards. The whistle blew and we looked around, wondering if it had been called an offside pass, but no: the Bruins had made a sloppy line change and Bob Myers, the referee, noted that the Bruins had six skaters on the ice.

With a Bruin in the box and just over a minute left in the game, Lafleur carried the puck out of our end and spotted Lemaire up by the Boston blue line. He fired the pass and then quickly followed the play. Coco dropped a pass back to Guy, who fired as hard a shot as I've ever seen. The shot was a laser, and it beat Gilles Gilbert, who fell over backwards and lay there as we celebrated tying the game. Don Cherry was devastated. The Bruins were crushed. They seemed to lose their spirit. It may be the most famous penalty in NHL history. The crucial penalty haunts Don Cherry to this day. In fact, he blamed himself for the penalty that ended the Bruins' hopes, and shortly afterwards, he was fired by Harry Sinden, Boston's general manager.

The game went into overtime, and Serge nicely broke up a Rick Middleton rush and passed the puck up to Mario Tremblay on the far side. Tremblay drove into the Bruins' end and, almost in the corner, fired a goalmouth pass that Yvon Lambert knocked in to send us back to the Stanley Cup final for a fourth straight spring.

Who could ever have dreamed a more outrageous script? That's why I think hockey is the best reality show imaginable. It was a classic series; one of the most intense of my career.

We still weren't finished, however. The Stanley Cup may be the hardest trophy in all of sports to win: you have to win 16 games before you can lay claim to it—and not one of those wins ever comes easily.

The final pitted us against the Rangers, starting with two games at the Forum in Montreal. Curiously, when we looked across at the Rangers' bench, behind it stood Fred "The Fog" Shero, our nemesis from the earlier Broad Street Bullies days. The Fog had been hired to coach the Rangers that season and had brought them to the final out of nowhere. He had them believing they could beat us to win the Cup.

Scotty knew that if we could throw Phil Esposito off his game, however, it would take away their momentum. Espo hated to be hit, so Scotty had Rod Langway give Phil the body every chance he could, and that strategy seemed to work. But the Rangers were checking hard too, and at one point Ken Hodge knocked me off my feet and I landed on my tailbone. That hurt like a son of a bitch. I could barely walk, let alone sit for a couple of weeks.

The Rangers won the first game, during which Scotty pulled Dryden after the second period and put in Bunny Larocque, who hadn't played in a playoff game with Montreal since 1974. Following the game, Scotty surprised us again and told us that Bunny would get the start in Game Two. We subscribed to the theory that you "dance with the one that brung ya," which was Kenny, of course, but you didn't argue with Scotty. But his strategy quickly fell apart when a Doug Risebrough shot during the warmup injured Larocque and he was unable to play. Kenny was suddenly back in goal, and was sensational the rest of the way. Bunny never again played a postseason game with the Canadiens.

We blew the Rangers out in that second game, and that really gave us confidence going into Madison Square Garden. We won 4–1 in Game Three, but the fourth game was much closer: at the end of regulation, we were tied at three apiece. About six minutes into extra time, I fired a shot that beat John Davidson in the Ranger net, but the goal light didn't go on and play didn't stop. Luckily, Serge scored right after and we won anyway, giving us a three-games-to-one lead in the series, which put a real stranglehold on the Rangers.

Game Five was the clincher. Played at the Forum, we beat them 4–1 to win our fourth Stanley Cup in a row. It was an amazing feeling: we were only the second team ever to put together four straight championships. The other was the 1950s Canadiens team with Jacques Plante, Doug Harvey, and the Rocket that ended up winning in five consecutive years. Missing from the celebration was Sam Pollock, whose name is not on the Stanley Cup for that season—but everybody appreciated that it was one more Stanley Cup for a team constructed by Sam.

Surprisingly, Montreal hadn't won the Stanley Cup on home ice since 1968, and it felt great to win it for our fans, who were as jubilant (maybe even more!) as we were. Serge Savard was handed the Stanley Cup as Yvan Cournoyer, in a suit, stood beside him, with all of us gathered around. We lifted the Cup high over our heads and skated the trophy around the perimeter of the ice to thank all of our loyal fans. The feeling never gets old, I can assure you.

It was announced that Bob Gainey had been awarded the Conn Smythe Trophy. A modest guy, he played such a key role in our victory. All battered and bruised, we lifted Bo onto our shoulders, and then he was handed the Stanley Cup. It was a golden moment.

Pierre Trudeau, the prime minister of Canada, had attended the game, and he joined us in the dressing room—amidst sweaty bodies, cheering teammates, and spraying champagne—to congratulate us.

After the traditional Stanley Cup parade, we went to celebrate together at Toe Blake's Tavern. Claude Mouton, who handled public relations for the Canadiens, was responsible for the Cup's safekeeping, but Guy Lafleur grabbed it and smuggled it into the trunk of his car. No one realized for a while that the Cup was missing while Flower drove to his parents' house in Thurso, Quebec, and displayed it on the front lawn, allowing his parents' neighbours and friends to enjoy the trophy with him. While Thurso was enjoying the celebration, Claude and others were searching frantically for the missing Cup, but Flower returned it later that night and was halfheartedly reprimanded. On the upside, he started a tradition: the idea for today's players getting the Stanley Cup for a day to celebrate actually came from Flower stealing the Cup that day.

CHAPTER 14

The Dynasty

"He had great teachers, he was a very smart player, and Larry learned to become very confident. Serge Savard was a great mentor for Larry through the years and Larry was a great student. Eventually, he passed the teacher."
– DOUG WILSON

Why were we so good for so long?

We were kids who grew up together, and we just loved playing together. Every one of us was drafted by the Canadiens except Kenny Dryden, Doug Jarvis, and Pete Mahovlich, though Dryden and Jarvis played their first NHL games with Montreal. Pete came to us in a trade with Detroit.

More importantly, we seemed to blossom at the same time. You could almost see it taking place. Guys finding their place in the lineup, finding their own strengths, gaining confidence with each shift. We didn't just play for a season or two with the same core of the team. We played five, six, seven years with the same guys. There was a sustained pattern of excellence. We were friends; we knew each other's families. We were very close as a team.

We also knew we were good. We knew that we had a team that could dominate and collect several Stanley Cup championships. We had great faith and trust in the abilities of each member of that team. We were skilled; we could skate, pass, check; we were tough; and then, we had Dryden back in goal. There are nine players from those teams that are now Honoured Members of the Hockey Hall of Fame: Cournoyer, Dryden, Gainey, Lafleur, Lapointe, Lemaire, Savard, Shutt, and me. Ten if you include Rod Langway. Plus, of course, Sam Pollock and Scotty Bowman, who joined the Hall in the Builders category.

We had a lot of fun together. Led Zeppelin boomed from our dressing room. Guy Lapointe was known to do just about anything for a laugh, and Pete Mahovlich was another one who kept the dressing room light. Shutty, Chartraw, and Risebrough were rah-rah guys. And then, we had the quiet leaders. Dryden kept very much to himself. So did Lafleur, Lemaire, and Savard. Gainey, too.

We were like a family. No matter who hosted the party, it wasn't uncommon to have almost everybody on the team there. We partied hard, but we played harder. That's just kind of how it was. When the Molsons owned the team, they usually gave us the Forum Club for our parties, and often supplied the beverages, too. We'd have Christmas parties, Hallowe'en, Thanksgiving—it was so much fun, and we'd all bring our wives.

There was a brasserie across the street from the Forum in the Alexis Nihon Plaza, and it was a ritual that when our morning practice was over, everybody would meet there. We'd have lunch and take turns buying rounds for the boys. We'd just sit around, yak and tell jokes, and then take off from there and go about our own business. If you weren't going to be there, you had to have a pretty darn good excuse.

After games, some of the younger guys went out on Crescent Street, which was a pretty notorious place to party. When I came to the team, I was already married and had a son, so I didn't really hang around with those guys. I was never a downtown Montreal nightlife guy. I had more friends on the West Island, so after a game, I usually went there and had dinner and a few beers with Jacques Lemaire and his wife.

Being drafted by the Montreal Canadiens was intimidating because they were so strong, especially on the blue line, and again, I wondered if I would ever get the chance to play. But it was the best thing that ever happened to me: I got to play with a great organization.

I was a tall, gangly kid when I first joined the Canadiens, but I found my rhythm. It takes a lot to get me upset about anything, and that hurt me early on in my career. It wasn't until I got a bit of a mean streak that my game started to elevate.

I tried to pick my spots, and that helped me establish my game. I didn't go looking for trouble, but if it came knocking, I'd be there. Intensity is what the game is about.

I had great teachers. In my first season, I played with Jacques Laperrière, an All-Star, Hall of Fame defenceman, and Lappy taught me a lot. Then, I was most fortunate to be paired with Serge Savard, and I can't say enough about him. I only became the player that I did because I got to play with Serge. I played seven years with him, and I made a lot of mistakes when we first started, but he always covered up for me. Serge had been a good rushing defenceman, but two separate occasions when he broke his leg changed his game. He evolved into an outstanding defensive defenceman, and as a result, we meshed well. We had full trust in each other and could read each other's mind. I knew that I could take off with the puck or follow the play, because Serge was going to be back to cover the zone should we lose possession. Many times, he saved my bacon.

Quite simply, Serge Savard is one of the most underrated players that I ever played with. When hockey fans talk about the best defencemen who ever played in that era, they always mention Bobby Orr and Brad Park—but if you look back, Serge should be right there with them. Sarge was an imposing figure, but his game was more cerebral, and he controlled the pace of the play.

We knew him as the Senator and as Sarge, and when he spoke, we all listened. He didn't talk often, but when he did, his presence commanded us to take notice. Sarge had a lot of business dealings outside of hockey. We were roommates and defence partners, but we didn't have anything in common outside the rink. Yet we had great admiration for each other. I never got to know Serge well, but if I asked him about legal matters, including contracts, he provided sage counsel.

The other member of our "Big Three" was Guy Lapointe, another underrated player. Pointu was great. He gave our team mobility—this guy played in every situation. He was on our power play, he could kill penalties, he was a good rushing defenceman, and he blocked shots. He was also the practical joker on the team. Once, Prime Minister Pierre Trudeau came into the dressing room after a game, moving from stall to stall and shaking hands with each of the guys. Guy stuck out his hand and the prime minister reared back quickly. Pointu had filled his hand with Vaseline!

If we were taking an escalator, Guy would be the first one on—and, inevitably, he would go and push the button to turn off the escalator so that the rest of us had to lug our suitcases up the stalled stairs. He was one of the funniest guys I've ever been associated with. If he had one knock, it was that he wasn't good at playing hurt—not that he didn't have a strong pain threshold. Maybe it's because he was such a perfectionist.

Rod Langway joined our defence corps in '78. I was able to act as a mentor to Rod when he joined us, but our relationship got off to anything but a smooth start. The French daily newspaper *La Presse* had a picture of Rod in training camp, but identified him as me. The two of us used to get mixed up quite often: we were both tall and slim with moustaches and similar hairstyles. Well, Rod occasionally got into trouble downtown—partying and staying out late. The next thing I knew, people were coming up to me and saying, "Larry, I saw you here" or "I saw you there" or "Who was that lady I saw you with?" I don't think so! I was home with my family. It caused me some problems. But Rod worked hard and became a really useful defenceman for us, and went on to become captain in Washington and won a couple of Norris Trophies.

Up ahead of us on the ice, our big scoring line was Coco (Jacques Lemaire) between Shutty (Steve Shutt) and Flower (Guy Lafleur). Everything that Guy did was natural. It was a pleasure just to go to practice and play with him. When anybody asks me my opinion on the best player I ever saw, right away, they expect me to say Gretzky or Lemieux, but I still think Flower is the best player I ever played with. Shutty and I are still very close friends. Even away from the rink, we hung around a lot because we played polo together in Montreal for a number of years. Steve was one of the best finishers that I probably played with: he had the best hand-eye coordination I've ever seen, being able to tip pucks in the air and that kind of stuff. It wasn't luck that he scored 60 goals in 1976–77—he was that good around the net.

What really made that line work, however, was Coco. Jacques Lemaire was an outstanding two-way centre, very responsible defensively and an amazing playmaker. I spent a bit of time in the summers with Lemaire. He had a place in Lac Labelle, and I'd take our family there. Jeannette and Michelle were very good friends, and our kids got along well.

Bob Gainey is a great friend—but of all of my friends, the one I know the least about. I don't know where he comes from, where he's going to, and I don't know what he's all about. He was a great player and a great competitor. Bob has gone through so much, losing his wife and losing his daughter. Another terrific person who went on to become a successful general manager with Minnesota, moving with them to Dallas, and then with Montreal.

There were so many guys who contributed to those Stanley Cup championships. At centre, we had Lemaire, Doug Jarvis, and Doug Risebrough. All brought different traits: Coco was, once again, a great two-way centre, Jarvis was an outstanding defensive centre, and Dougie Risebrough had the feistiness. Scotty could throw any of them out to play against the top lines of the other teams. Other guys brought much-needed energy, like Mario Tremblay and Yvon Lambert.

Kenny Dryden, though, was a different guy. He liked to be alone, and we left him alone. Kenny seldom attended dinners or parties with the rest of the team, but on the ice, we always knew he was there for us. If we were behind by a goal or two with five minutes to go, Scotty would tell Serge, Guy Lapointe, or me to rush the puck and pinch at their blue line, because we were all confident with Kenny back there in net. He didn't get a lot of shots, but when he did, he was right there. He had incredible focus. The mental part of his game was so strong; Kenny is a really cerebral guy. I've played in front of Patrick Roy and coached Martin Brodeur, and aside from those two, Kenny is probably the best goaltender that I've ever seen.

Scotty himself was the right coach for our team during those years. He was a master who kept our interest level high and knew how to get us ready each night. He knew when to play certain guys and when to let up on guys. He could get the best out of a player, but he always kept us off balance. There were nights that I used to have nightmares about Scotty. I wanted to choke him. The problem is, that's what he wanted. There'd be games where we won by five or six goals, and the next day, he'd blast the living hell out of us, telling us we played a horrible game. Then we'd practise for half an hour, and with a big smile on his face, he'd tell us that was it and send us home. You could never figure him out. He was always trying to stay one step ahead.

I think Scotty was the best bench coach who was ever involved in hockey. Steve Shutt said Scotty was hated by the team 364 days of the year, but we all loved him on that day when we won the Stanley Cup.

CHAPTER 15

Larry, Moe . . . and Surly

"Unless you have that shiny Cup at the end of the season, then it isn't what you call a successful year. In Montreal, you lead a pressure-filled life. You're like an actor—always in the spotlight. And if you let the pressure of playing at the Forum torture you, you'll drive yourself crazy and be ready to retire after two or three years. But when you win the Stanley Cup, that's worth all the aches and aggravation."

— LARRY ROBINSON

I don't really like the term *dynasty,* although I understand why people regard the success that we enjoyed in that way. We won four consecutive Stanley Cup championships, and all the press could do was draw parallels between our team and the team of the 1950s that won five in a row.

The 1970s were Sam Pollock's decade, no question. And after Sam retired, most people, including Scotty Bowman, had thought that Scotty would be named general manager. There is no doubt that he wanted the position. But everyone was surprised when the new owners passed on Scotty and named Irving Grundman the GM.

Irving had been president of the Forum during the Bronfman era and was a very successful businessman. I guess the Molsons figured that that was what the franchise needed at the time. And don't forget that the team had a lot of good hockey people around to help Irving, too. But even though we had won the Stanley Cup that spring of 1979, everything started to change that summer.

Teams go through their own evolution. Players leave and new ones replace them. It's hard to see some go, and to others, it's not quite as difficult to say goodbye. It's just the way the game goes, but with every change in personnel, a team changes too. And with each coaching change, the team changes that much more.

I was with the Canadiens for another 10 years after that Stanley Cup in 1979, and by the time I pulled on that Montreal sweater for the last time, only Bob Gainey and I were left from those teams that had enjoyed so much success.

Not only had our captain, Yvan Cournoyer, been forced to retire due to his back problems, but Kenny Dryden hadn't enjoyed the 1978–79 season in spite of winning the Cup. He decided he wanted to pursue a career outside of hockey and left the game to explore new challenges. Jacques Lemaire, who scored the Cup-winning goal in 1979, left the Canadiens after that season to pursue a coaching career in Switzerland.

Meanwhile, Rick Chartraw was traded to Los Angeles for a draft pick in February 1981, Bunny Larocque was traded to Toronto in March, and the Senator, Serge Savard, joined the Winnipeg Jets in October of that year. Yvon Lambert was picked up on waivers by the Buffalo Sabres in 1981, and Pierre Larouche was traded away to Hartford in December.

Guy Lapointe was dealt to the St. Louis Blues for a draft pick in March 1982, and a trade with Washington in September '82 sent Brian Engblom, Dougie Jarvis, and Rod Langway to the Capitals. Doug Risebrough was traded to the Calgary Flames for draft picks that same month, and we'd meet up with him again in an important playoff series.

Reggie Houle retired in September 1983, and Mark Napier was dealt to Edmonton a month later. Steve Shutt went to the Kings in November '84. The next year, Pierre Mondou suffered an eye injury that forced him to retire in March 1985, and Flower retired—at least temporarily—at the end of that season. Mario Tremblay suffered an injury to his shoulder and retired in March 1986.

And through that decade of player changes, we had *seven* different coaches. You can imagine that each one had a different style, a different personality, and as players, we had to adjust.

At the beginning of that stretch, Scotty Bowman had struggled to work under Grundman and left at the end of the 1978–79 season. At his media conference, he stated, "There was no room for Irving Grundman and me on the same team. I was convinced that I had the competence to be general manager, and I couldn't tolerate the way Grundman directed the club. He said he had a lot of respect for me as a coach. I had some for him as a businessman, but I have no respect for him as a hockey man, and I couldn't continue in this way. It was better for them and me that I go. It was a question of hockey philosophy."

Scotty, who was the only coach I had played for in Montreal, left us to join the Buffalo Sabres as their coach and general manager. It was a great opportunity for him, although I'm sure he would have preferred to stay with the Canadiens. Bernie Geoffrion was hired to replace Scotty. Boom had coached the New York Rangers and Atlanta Flames, so he had coaching experience, and of course, he was one of the great players in the history of the Montreal Canadiens. But he had quit coaching both teams because of the pressures of the job, and here he was, facing the extraordinary pressure of being under the microscope in Montreal.

Boom lost control of the team. He knew what he wanted us to do, but he couldn't get his message across to the guys. He was too casual, especially after we were used to Scotty's ways. Pre-game meetings with Scotty started at 6:30 sharp and ran up to 30 minutes, preparing us thoroughly for the game that night. Under Geoffrion, most pre-game meetings started at 6:30 and ended by 6:32. His favourite line was, "I don't have to tell you guys what to do. Go out there and do your job."

Things went sour quickly. One of the big issues was over Boom's son, Danny. He was a member of the team and had some skills, but Claude Ruel (as director of player development) didn't want him in the lineup and ordered Geoffrion not to dress him. Boom couldn't handle the interference from Claude, and after only 30 games, he quit. "I had a dream to coach this team," he said at the time. "That dream is a nightmare now. I don't care if you pay me a million dollars, I will not stay."

And he didn't.

Claude Ruel reluctantly agreed to return as head coach. He was a great hockey man who had filled in as coach on a couple of previous occasions. Sarge was named captain of the team. He was a leader in every way, and we were all pleased with that decision. Meanwhile, though Boom Boom had experimented with me at left wing for a while, I was quite pleased to return to the blue line.

It wasn't all doom and gloom. We still occasionally made our own fun. Mark Hebscher, a television personality working in Hamilton, Ontario, reminded me of an April Fool's prank we pulled in the spring of 1980. I was scheduled to be interviewed on the first of April by Mark, who was the morning sports announcer on FM96 Radio in Montreal at the time. But rather than agreeing to the usual interview (where I'd be asked for the thousandth time if we could win a fifth straight Stanley Cup in spite of losing Bowman, Dryden, etc.), I asked him if he had made any plans to pull a prank on his FM96 radio listeners. It turned out that he had not, so I suggested one.

That morning, thousands of Canadiens fans woke up to learn that I had been traded to the Los Angeles Kings for Marcel Dionne. I'm a pretty modest guy, but I have to admit that my performance that morning was Oscar-worthy. I sobbed on the air as I thanked the great fans of Montreal for years of support. I concluded the mock interview with, "I'm numb. I want to thank the fans for all the great years in Montreal, and now I'm going to hitch my boat to my truck and head out to L.A. Thank you, everybody." I pretended that I couldn't continue, that the emotion had overwhelmed me.

The phones in the newsroom of the radio station lit up like a Christmas tree. The word spread like wildfire, and other radio stations started to report the trade, too. Claude Ruel, our coach, even called me once I got home. He was livid and wanted to find out what was going on, oblivious to the fact that it was April Fool's Day.

The radio station played the interview several times, but by the end of Mark's shift at 9:00 that morning, he had to let the listeners in on the joke. "April Fool's, everybody! Larry Robinson isn't going anywhere. In fact, this prank was his idea!"

We had a good chuckle and thought that was the end of the joke. But it wasn't. A newspaper reporter, hearing the story on the radio, had called Marcel Dionne, waking him up at 3:30 a.m. to get his reaction to the big trade. "What trade?" he asked. He was told that he was part of a deal sending him to Montreal in exchange for Larry Robinson. Marcel was in complete shock, and nervously waited on a call from the Kings to confirm the trade. And then he realized what day it was.

We had pulled off a great April Fool's prank. I guess Marcel cornered Hebscher at a golf tournament and through gritted teeth said, "You're the son of a bitch that traded me for Larry Robinson, aren't you?" He then laughed and added, "Robinson wasn't enough. It would have been more believable if you had the Canadiens include a draft pick, too."

Actually, I thought it was a pretty good trade straight up. That season, I won the Norris Trophy and Marcel won the Art Ross as the NHL's scoring leader.

But it wasn't the only highlight of that year: another wonderful thing was for me to see my younger brother get the chance to play with the Canadiens, even though it was only for one game.

Moe had been drafted by the Canadiens in 1977 and attended four Montreal training camps, but each time had been sent down to Halifax to play for the Voyageurs in the American Hockey League. I remember the first training camp he came to, where one writer said it looked like "somebody brought along a stick with red tape on the top of the handle." He was a tall, scrawny kid, like I had been when I attended my first camp. I felt sorry for him because he was never considered on his own merits—he was always Larry Robinson's little brother. I tried to stay out of the way as much as possible so that he could come and make it his own way.

Moe had to do the same thing I did and earn his stripes, and I know he did everything that was asked of him. The AHL was a tough league, and there were fights almost every night. Moe fought some of the toughest guys and did really well. I knew he wasn't very big, but he was a tough customer.

When I was injured in December 1979, they called Moe up and he got to play a few shifts, but they sent him back down. There was a time later in the season when they wanted to call him up as an injury replacement, but he was hurt and unable to play.

I don't think the Canadiens gave him a true shot to make it. He was sent to Oklahoma City (Minnesota's farm team) the next year and played there for a season. He had a great time there and loved the city. I went with him to ask Mr. Grundman if he could arrange a trade with the North Stars, because he was property of the Canadiens and it was clear he wasn't going to get a chance to play in Montreal. Mr. Grundman said he would try to make a deal, but after Minnesota made an offer, the Canadiens turned it down. Moe got discouraged and got out of hockey after that. That was a travesty, because he could have been a very good minor-league player, and if he had been traded to the North Stars organization, he might have been called up at some point and could have done a nice job there.

Moe ended up going back to school and got his mechanic's licence. He's been a mechanic for years and years, and owns a shop back home in Marvelville. At one point, when I owned a garage in Montreal, Moe worked for us for five or six years. He still occasionally plays hockey with the Ottawa Senators alumni.

In spite of the changes, the 1980 Canadiens had a productive season. It was impossible to replace Dryden in goal, and we missed Coco Lemaire's work in both ends of the rink, but we finished first in our division, and for the sixth season in a row, we reached the 100-point plateau.

In the playoffs, we easily eliminated the Hartford Whalers, but got knocked out in the second round in seven games by those Minnesota North Stars after injuries had decimated our lineup.

Hopes of winning five Cups in a row had evaporated pretty quickly. It was a devastating conclusion to a terribly discouraging season. We were also about to start a Stanley Cup drought that, while short for any other city, would seem interminable in Montreal.

CHAPTER 16

The Battles of Quebec

"Robinson cruises the ice as a belligerent peacemaker, going nose to nose and stare to stare with anyone who threatens a teammate." – KEN DRYDEN (in *The Game*)

In 1980–81, we finished the season with more than 100 points for the seventh consecutive time. In the last half of the season, we only lost once at home, so we felt pretty confident going into the playoffs. But we ran into a young Edmonton Oilers team in the opening round. Although it would take them a few years to fully mature, they still were a very, very good team, and they beat us in three straight to end our Stanley Cup hopes.

Just a few days after our season ended, Claude Ruel resigned as our head coach. At that summer's draft, Irving Grundman announced that Bob Berry would be his replacement as head coach of the Canadiens. Bob had played for L.A., and after retiring, he had coached there, too. He was a Montreal native and could speak both French and English.

That summer, John Ferguson, who was general manager of the Winnipeg Jets, convinced Serge to join his team. That was disappointing to me on a personal level, as we had been defence partners through some very successful years and had been roommates on the road, too. After that, I was paired on the blue line with every young guy they brought up to the team. Sarge had also been our captain, and Bob Gainey was given the captaincy to replace Savard.

Meanwhile, both Flower and I were negotiating new contracts at the same time. Norm Caplan, our agent, decided to negotiate in tandem. Although Sam Pollock was no longer with the club, he had always said that the Canadiens' policy was simple: you had to earn your stardom, and then would be paid accordingly. We both had proved our worth to the Montreal Canadiens over and over, and wanted to be rewarded in kind. It took some negotiating, but we were both quite pleased with the result.

Back on the ice, we had a lot of depth at centre. Keith Acton, Doug Jarvis, Pierre Larouche, Pierre Mondou, Doug Risebrough, and Doug Wickenheiser were all centres and all looking for ice time—but there was only so much space. Even though Larouche had been a 50-goal scorer for us, he and Grundman clashed and, just before Christmas, Pierre was sent to the Hartford Whalers for a first-round pick in the 1984 draft.

Through the 1970s, sportswriters had referred to Serge, Guy, and me as the Big Three, but Serge had moved on to Winnipeg and, in March 1982, Pointu was traded to St. Louis. I understand that it's the nature of the game, but slowly, our Montreal Canadiens "family" was disappearing. Things can never stay the same, even though you wish they could go on forever.

I was very pleased to be named to the Second All-Star Team in 1981–82, and the Canadiens finished third overall, again collecting more than 100 points. In the first round of the playoffs, we faced the Quebec Nordiques. There was no love lost between us and the Nordiques. We finished substantially higher than they did during the regular season, but passion rose to the surface whenever our teams met.

This was the first time the two Quebec teams met in the post-season since the Nordiques joined the NHL. We split the first two games of the best-of-five series, played at the Forum. The next two games were played at Le Colisée in Quebec City, where, in Game Three, Dale Hunter scored both goals and they beat us 2–1 to go up two games to one in the series. Game Four got heated quickly, and a brawl broke out in the first period that lasted 20 minutes and involved every player from both teams. When the smoke cleared, there was something like 150 penalty minutes assessed and a few guys given game misconducts. We won that one 6–2.

The deciding game was played back home at the Forum. The Nordiques took a first-period lead with two goals, but we came back and tied the game in the third period. The game went into over-time, and Dale Hunter ended our season less than a minute into the extra period when he and Real Cloutier combined for a con-troversial goal. At first, the goal light didn't go on, but the referee indicated it was in. After trying to console our goalie, Rick Wamsley, we shook hands with the Nordiques and took off our equipment for another season.

•

More surprises were in store in the personnel department, and I was stunned when, just before the start of the 1982–83 season, Irving Grundman traded Brian Engblom, Doug Jarvis, Rod Langway, and Craig Laughlin to the Washington Capitals for Rick Green and Ryan Walter. I thought we gave up too much in the trade, which stemmed from Langway being unhappy with his contract. Grundman emphasized, "Rod made it clear to us that if he was not traded to an American team, he was going to retire." Rod had been very solid on defence, a good shot-blocking defensive defenceman who would go on to star with the Capitals, but I actually thought we missed Englblom even more. He had been our best defenceman in '81–82 and was an All-Star that year.

If nothing else, though, we were consistent in 1982–83, finishing second in the Adams Division, just shy of the 100-point plateau. We faced the Buffalo Sabres in the first round of the playoffs, and even though they lagged behind us during the regular season, they swept us in three straight games.

I had been infuriated at one point during the year when Berry told the media that we were leaderless on the ice and pointed out me and Flower specifically. Those shots hurt. You try to shake them off and rationalize that a coach is just trying to motivate his team, but when it becomes personal like that, you take offence and never feel quite the same about the guy.

The franchise was in a slow decline and all of us players knew that a change was likely to take place, but we were quite surprised when Ronald Corey, the team president, fired Irving Grundman as well as Ron Caron, the director of player personnel, and didn't renew the contract of coach Bob Berry. I had figured that either Grundman or Berry would be fired, but was surprised that both were. I felt sorry for Bob because, overall, he had been a fair and good coach.

Serge Savard still had an option year on his contract with the Winnipeg Jets, but when the Canadiens offered him the GM position, he retired from playing and accepted the job, replacing Grundman. And, much to our surprise, one of Serge's first moves was to rehire Bob Berry.

In defence of Grundman, we did draft some really good players during his time with the team. Guy Carbonneau, Mats Näslund, Craig Ludwig, and Chris Chelios were all selected while he was GM, although there was the controversial draft in 1980 when we picked Doug Wickenheiser, when the popular selection would have been Denis Savard.

We picked up Claude Lemieux in the draft that summer of 1983, and in October, Serge traded for Bobby Smith from Minnesota. Poor Doug Wickenheiser, who was a lightning rod for the resentment of fans and media alike, was dealt to St, Louis during the season. But 1983–84 was still disappointing, as we tumbled in the standings and finished fourth in our division, more than 20 points behind the previous season. And despite rehiring Berry, Serge decided to re-fire him partway through the season, as we were really struggling. Berry let his frustrations get the best of him, screaming at us in a bid to motivate the team. It didn't work, as the guys just tuned him out. "Never in my seven years of coaching have I seen a team as tough to motivate," he told the press. Replacing him was an old friend, and a secret weapon from many of our most successful teams: Jacques Lemaire was moved into the head coaching position. We went on a nice run in the playoffs, first sweeping the Bruins before we met the Nordiques in the second round.

Again we split the first two games, this time played at Le Colisée. We took Game Three at home, but Quebec edged us in overtime in Game Four to tie up the series. We came back with a dominant 4–0 win in Game Five in Quebec City.

And then there was Game Six.

They call it the Good Friday Massacre, and it truly was a debacle. The game was televised across Canada and the United States on April 20, 1984. The puck had barely been dropped when Mike McPhee and Wilf Paiement got into a fight. There were a number of small scraps after that, and you could feel it building. Dale Hunter was running Steve Penney all night, and we weren't going to allow that—but Hunter wasn't easily intimidated.

We were down 1–0 near the end of the second period, when a little pushing and shoving began to the left of Quebec's goalie, Dan Bouchard, just before the battle broke out. And did it break out!

As the period ended, Hunter drove Guy Carbonneau into the ice, which prompted Chris Nilan to go in to defend Carbo. At that point, the benches cleared, so there were 40 guys swarming all over the ice, and the three officials could only do so much. Mario Tremblay punched Peter Stastny and broke his nose. Louie Sleigher of the Nordiques hammered Jean Hamel, who was tied up by a linesman and not expecting to be hit, knocking him unconscious. Everybody else paired off—even the backup goalies fought.

After quite a long period of time, tempers cooled enough to get both teams to their dressing rooms. Referee Bruce Hood had to delay the start of the third period so he could tally up all the infractions. A bunch of guys were tossed and a ton of penalties were assessed. But what occurred next was inexplicable: when the third period was set to begin, all the players from both teams came out to warm up. No one had been notified about who had been ejected and who had been penalized (although it was pretty evident to all of us), so everyone was on the ice—and a *second* brawl started, including all the guys who should have been out of the game. It was absurd! Sleigher was back on the ice after annihilating Hamel, and that was BS, so we went right after him. Mark Hunter, who played for us, swung his stick at Sleigher, and the next thing I knew, Mark was fighting his brother, Dale. Paiement and I got into a fight as well. By the time order had been restored, almost an hour had gone by since we had last played.

In the end, 12 players had been ejected from the game and 252 penalty minutes were assessed. It was an embarrassment. Rivalries are one thing, but the Good Friday Massacre was something else altogether. Both teams barely had enough players to complete the game, but shortly after the Nordiques took a 2–0 lead, we roared back and scored five. The game ended in a 5–3 win for us, which gave us the victory in the series—and in the battle of Quebec.

Our next matchup was against the New York Islanders for the Prince of Wales Trophy as champions of the east, but I have to think that we were physically and mentally exhausted from our series with the Nordiques. The Islanders eliminated us in six games and went on to the Stanley Cup final—a rematch against the Edmonton Oilers. The Islanders hoped to match the Montreal Canadiens' record of five consecutive Stanley Cup championships, but were halted by the upstart Oilers, who won their franchise's first-ever Stanley Cup championship.

CHAPTER 17

Return to Glory

"Larry was always the first one on the ice. He was great around the guys, always making jokes and relaxing everybody. We called him 'Big Bird' and I used to think he was the oldest teenager on the team." – JEAN PERRON (in Dick Irvin's *Behind the Bench*)

Despite the exodus of players from our dynasty years, there were still a handful of us veterans left with the team. Bob Gainey was captain, of course, but Mario Tremblay and I were named alternate captains. We had already taken on leadership roles with the team, but to be recognized with the A was a real honour.

As GM, Serge made his mark pretty quickly at the 1984 draft. He sent Rick Wamsley and three draft picks to the St. Louis Blues for two draft picks, and with them picked up Shayne Corson and Stéphane Richer. That draft also saw the Canadiens select Petr Svoboda in the first round, and in the third round: Patrick Roy. I don't think anyone had any idea just how good Patrick would be. He spent most of the season back in junior, but was called up in February for his first NHL game. That season was Chris Chelios's first full season in the NHL, too.

In the meantime, I had started to doubt myself a little. Lemaire was playing me less than what I was used to, giving additional playing time to younger guys like Chelios and Craig Ludwig. And I was getting booed at times by our own fans, which preys on a player's head. It hurt, and there were nights when I didn't sleep much. There were other nights when I just had an extra beer to help put me to sleep. Hard times, to be sure, but you have to take the good with the bad—and if I was honest with myself, there were nights when I simply didn't play well. Maybe it was age catching up with me, or maybe it was because I had too many things going on off the ice, and I wasn't making hockey my sole priority. It happens. We weren't making the salaries that the guys today make, so players were always looking for other ways to make extra money, and in some cases, to prepare us for life after retirement.

From the time I was climbing aboard tractors back home on the farm, I had a love of vehicles, and as I got to driving age, I really had an affection for beautiful cars. There was a place around the corner from the Forum called Dingy's, named after John Dingman, who was one of the owners and the head mechanic. Dingy's used to service the Zambonis. Mechanically, John was brilliant: he'd take an engine apart and put it back together in a weekend. Cars were definitely his passion. The other owner was Donny Cape, a guy the Grundmans knew. I would occasionally take my vehicle in to Dingy's to have work done because they did great work and I really liked the guys. I started to hang out there in the mid-'70s, and spending time at Dingy's took my mind off of hockey. I could walk over there, learn a bit more about cars, and dabble a little.

I had always wanted a Corvette. When I went looking for one, Donny helped me find a beautiful vintage Corvette convertible. I took it to Dingy's, and with a bit of help from me, they fixed it up beautifully. What a gorgeous car!

A few years later, when Dingy's was looking into moving to a new location on Paré, near the Blue Bonnets Raceway (later the Hippodrome de Montréal), I asked if they were interested in another partner. They actually resisted at first, as I wasn't a mechanic and they didn't need an investor, but we finally worked out a deal and the three of us ended up buying the place. We spent some nights renovating the space, and I had an office built there and ran my personal company out of that spot. My brother Moe worked there as a mechanic as well. When I wasn't playing or practising, I ended up going to the shop, dabbling away, learning about cars and chatting with customers. Donny Cape is still my dear friend and business advisor all these years later.

•

After a season of uncertainty, I showed up at training camp in 1984 with a new appreciation and confidence after playing in the Canada Cup in September. That team had guys like Glenn Anderson, Paul Coffey, and Mark Messier—they could frigging fly! I said to myself, "You know what? I can still skate with those guys." That really helped me put things into perspective, and I came back from the Canada Cup in the best shape of my life. I started feeling good about myself again, and I ended up having a really strong season.

Back then, the preseason was every bit as competitive as the playoffs. Furthermore, we met the Bruins in an exhibition game in October 1984, and there were always fireworks any time we played Boston. In this game, Chris Nilan and Terry O'Reilly—two big, tough boys—got into a fight, and the next thing I knew, I caught Brian Curran out of the corner of my eye going after Chelios. I turned to grab him so he couldn't get at Cheli, but he landed on top of me and I lost my balance, hitting the back of my head on the ice. I was out cold. Brian saw all the blood and rushed over to the Montreal bench to get the trainer, but my teammates thought he was coming over to challenge them to fight. I don't remember going down at all. All I know is that when I came to, I was in the dressing room getting a bunch of stitches.

I was back in action shortly, but other changes were happening around me. Steve Shutt was traded to Los Angeles near the start of the 1984–85 season, and while we were very close, I was happy for him. L.A. was where he wanted to go, and Serge accommodated him. A month later, Guy Lafleur played his final game with the Canadiens. He had struggled the last season or so, and where plays had always come to him intuitively, I sensed that he now had to think about which move to make. He was such a star, and everybody wanted to see the same Flower of the mid-70s, flying down the ice, his hair flying behind him—but those days were no more. Flower had only scored two goals to that point in the season and wasn't happy with the ice time he was getting. Unbeknownst to his teammates, Guy was mulling over his future in hockey. Twenty games into the season, we were about to fly to Boston when we were informed that Flower had a sore ankle and wouldn't be making the trip. In actuality, he had decided that he was through, and two days later, he announced his retirement at a media conference. I'm a pretty sentimental guy, and have to admit that the retirement of one of the greatest ever to play the game—and one of the greatest teammates I ever had played with—got me quite emotional. Guy and I had been drafted by the Canadiens on the same day. It was the end of an era.

We finished first in the Adams Division in 1984–85, just ahead of Quebec and Buffalo. After beating the Bruins in the opening round of the playoffs, we faced the Nordiques once again: it seemed we couldn't get away from them. In the spring of 1982, they had eliminated us, but in 1984, we beat them. We thought we should be able to handle them easily in 1985 after beating them six times and tying them once in the eight games we played against each other that season. But the Nordiques won the first and third games in overtime en route to a seventh and deciding game. After regulation, we were still tied 2–2! But overtime haunted us again, as Peter Stastny scored early in the extra period to give the Nordiques the series.

•

Jacques Lemaire resigned as head coach that summer of 1985 and was given the role of director of hockey personnel. The decision really threw the team for a loop, and I had no inkling that he was even thinking of resigning—but knowing Jacques the way I did, that wasn't unusual. He was always very good at keeping things to himself.

Jacques suggested that assistant coach Jean Perron be made the head coach. Jean had been with us in 1984–85 and had been a successful coach with the University of Moncton's hockey team as well as an assistant with Canada's Olympic team. But he had no NHL experience. I never really felt like I connected with Jean. He was a very nice man—he was fair and he worked hard—but I never got a handle on him.

We started the 1985–86 season with a rookie coach overseeing a lineup filled with rookies. Guys like Kjell Dahlin, Sergio Momesso, Stéphane Richer, Patrick Roy, and Brian Skrudland had all joined our roster that season. Early on, Jean called a meeting of his veterans, asking for our support, which we vowed to give him. The problem, though, was that as the season went on, guys realized that Jean wasn't able to instill discipline, so they openly defied him—which is a death sentence for any coach.

Lemaire both nurtured and challenged us, but Perron's style resulted in tumultuous relationships with a few of the players and some of the staff. Notable was a very public feud with Chris Nilan, which resulted in Nilan getting traded to the Rangers after a confrontation with the coach.

Our lineup was frequently juggled, partly due to injury but partly to find some chemistry, and as a result, nobody knew which Montreal Canadiens team was going to show up on any given night. We would go into Philadelphia or Long Island and whip the Flyers and the Islanders (both tough teams), but then we'd lose home games to weaker squads like Minnesota or Los Angeles.

There was a divide in the team, and we had lost confidence in Perron. Late in the season, I couldn't hold back any longer: after Jean put us through a 90-minute practice that left us panting, I asked Red Fisher of the Montreal *Gazette*, "Is he telling us that we're out if shape after 73 games of the regular season? Losing games is a problem, so we've got problems. We've got a lot of problems. And the only way you solve problems is to get some discipline on the ice." I guess he wanted to show us how tough he could be, but if he wanted respect from the players, he had to respect us, too.

The media swirled with stories about Perron's imminent firing, and we had players-only meetings to try to sort things out. Finally, Serge Savard and Jacques Lemaire called a meeting where Serge made it abundantly clear that there would be no coaching change and that he was committed to Jean Perron.

We finished behind the first-place Nordiques in the Adams Division that season, and things weren't all bad. Mats Näslund had

Kevin Shea

Marvelville is a farming community in the Ottawa Valley, southeast of Canada's capital. The village is too small to support a hospital, so I was born at the nearby Winchester District Memorial Hospital on June 2, 1951.

I attended Grades 1 through 8 at the tiny U.S.S. No. 5 Russell in Marvelville. These days, it is the village's community centre, where they have a display chronicling my career.

Kevin Shea

Larry Robinson Collection

I was in Grade 8 at U.S.S. No. 5 Russell when this class picture was taken in 1964; I'm in the back row, fourth from the left.

Le Studio du Hockey/Hockey Hall of Fame

I was converted from forward to defence during my two seasons (1968–69 and 1969–70) with the Brockville Braves of the Central Junior 'A' Hockey League.

Kevin Shea

My one season with the Kitchener Rangers in 1970-71 couldn't have been more challenging. I was struggling to work full-time and play junior while newly married and raising a newborn. Yet, somehow, I managed to get drafted by the Montreal Canadiens that season.

Graphic Artists/Hockey Hall of Fame

I credit Al MacNeil, Claude Ruel and Noel Price for really helping me develop into an NHL-ready defenceman while playing with the Canadiens' American Hockey League affiliate, the Nova Scotia Voyageurs. We won the Calder Cup championship in 1971–72.

Hockey Hall of Fame

After starting the 1972–73 season in the AHL, I was summoned to join the Canadiens and played my first NHL game on January 8, 1973 against the Minnesota North Stars.

Hockey Hall of Fame

Serge Savard was the one who tagged me 'Big Bird,' one of those nicknames that has stuck with me to this day.

Focus on Sport/Getty Images

The Canadiens faced the Bruins in the Stanley Cup final for a second straight spring in 1978. We beat them in a tough six-game series to win our third consecutive Stanley Cup.

Denis Brodeur/Larry Robinson Collection

That spring was special for many reasons. I was also named winner of the Conn Smythe Trophy as the most valuable player in the playoffs.

Larry Robinson Collection

We won four consecutive Stanley Cup championships in the 1970s, but it wasn't just the players and management who celebrated these victories. The wives were every bit as much a part of our success, and enjoyed the celebrations as much as we did.

Lewis Portnoy/Hockey Hall of Fame

While I was fortunate to have been a six-time All-Star and twice won the Norris Trophy, team success was always far more important to me. Winning the Stanley Cup six times as a player is my career highlight.

Hockey Hall of Fame

I was honoured to represent my country on many occasions. Some were classic series and others, not so much. I played with cracked ribs and a sprained wrist against the Soviet Red Army on New Year's Eve in 1979 in a game that was nowhere as exciting as our contest on New Year's Eve 1975.

Graphic Artists/Hockey Hall of Fame

My brother Moe was a really good hockey player and played one game with the Canadiens during the 1979–80 season, ironically, replacing me following an injury.

Denis Brodeur Collection/Club de hockey Canadien, Inc.

My love of cars led me to Dingy's, a garage down the street from the Forum where I could clear my mind of hockey by tinkering with automobiles. I later bought into the business. My brother Moe (left) became a mechanic. That's John 'Dingy' Dingman in the centre.

Many Millan/Sports Illustrated/Getty Images

Besides the Cup wins, I am most proud of my career plus/minus record, which is +730. In 1976–77, I was +120. Only Bobby Orr and I have had a plus/minus rating of +100 or greater in a season.

Miles Nadal/Hockey Hall of Fame

After winning my second Norris Trophy in 1979–80, I was asked to present the trophy for the NHL's best defenceman to the 1980–81 recipient, Randy Carlyle.

James Lipa/Hockey Hall of Fame

The Canada Cup series of 1981 was an embarrassment. Not only did Canada lose badly to the Soviets, but most of the team went home, leaving me and Gretz to sit at the head table of the post-tournament banquet with Alan Eagleson and Canadian Prime Minister Pierre Trudeau.

Frank Prazak/Hockey Hall of Fame

I got the reputation for delivering big hits, but I was occasionally on the receiving end, as I was here with Jim Schoenfeld of the Buffalo Sabres.

a sensational year and Patrick Roy was outstanding. We hadn't had that kind of confidence in a goaltender since Kenny Dryden was with the team. Ryan Walter broke his ankle in late March, which opened a spot for Pepé (Claude) Lemieux, but Ryan came back just six weeks later to play in the final.

Through the previous couple of seasons, I had occasionally experienced the slings and arrows of the fans, who expected me to be Superman at times. But just like the Canada Cup year, I felt rejuvenated in 1985–86 and had one of the best seasons of my career. I ended up scoring 19 goals and had 82 points and was named to the NHL's Second All-Star Team.

Our path to the Stanley Cup final took us through Boston, where we swept the Bruins. My old "friend" Louie Sleigher, now with the Bruins, ran over Patrick Roy behind our net, and I took some pleasure in making him accountable for his actions. John Kordic laid his own licking on Jay Miller, and Claude Lemieux scored some important goals for us.

We defeated Hartford next in a tough seven-game series, with Lemieux scoring the seventh-game overtime winner. Now our confidence was high—forget about the speed bumps during the season, we knew we could go all the way. We beat the Rangers in five games to win the Prince of Wales Conference final, which set up a Stanley Cup final against the Calgary Flames. We had gotten a huge break when the Flames eliminated the Oilers in the Campbell Conference final, though the Flames were no slouches themselves. This set up the first all-Canadian Stanley Cup final since I was back home in Marvelville, watching Toronto and Montreal play for the Cup in 1967.

The Flames surprised us in Game One, outscoring us 5–2. We edged the Flames 3–2 in the second game, which was decided after just nine seconds of overtime, when Brian Skrudland scored to win the game. We won 5–3 in Game Three, and then Patrick shut out the Flames 1–0 in Game Four.

Game Five turned out to be the deciding game for us. We took the ice at the Olympic Saddledome in Calgary with our eyes on the prize. It was close—closer than we would have liked—as the Flames scored twice late in the game to come within a goal of tying us. I sensed panic, so took it upon myself to try to calm the guys down. The Flames still almost tied it up with seconds to go, but Patrick made the save to preserve the win. We had ridden Bobby Smith's goal midway through the third to a 4–3 win . . . and the Stanley Cup!

When the final buzzer sounded, I immediately searched the ice for my longtime teammate Bob Gainey, and then I looked over to where Serge sat and gave him a nod and a smile. He knew how special that win was. For both of us. When the Stanley Cup was handed to Bob, I got emotional. And then, when he handed the Cup to me, I wept like a baby.

They awarded the Conn Smythe Trophy to Patrick Roy, who had been a wall in the net for us. Any concerns about a rookie starting for us in the postseason had long since been eliminated. I can say without hesitation that we would not have won this Stanley Cup without Patrick.

I looked around the dressing room: a lot of guys contributed to this victory. Mats Näslund led us in scoring in the final. Pepé Lemieux was feisty and opened up a lot of space for our guys. Guy Carbonneau threw himself in front of shot after shot. After a couple of seasons where I didn't always enjoy going to the rink, I competed hard and enjoyed myself again, and was able to contribute in a significant way. I hadn't told anyone (except the trainers), but my elbow was a mess. I had an inflammation of the bursal sac, and every time I banged it, the damn thing swelled up like a balloon. I had had to have it drained after every game.

Of course, any time you accomplish your goal—in this case, winning the Stanley Cup—you forget about the aches and pains and can only think about the incredible fun. Especially once the series is over.

This was my sixth Stanley Cup championship. Just like with children, you can't pick a favourite, but I must admit that this victory was sweet, especially because it was unexpected. We got hot at the right time and rode a great young goaltender to the win. It felt especially good because guys like me and Bo were the only remnants left from those wins in the 1970s. We had a special bond. Our wives were like two peas in a pod. And Gainey and I both hated losing. We did whatever we could to win hockey games. Bo was a great man who never spoke a lot, but when he did, you listened. That's probably why he was such a good captain. He was our leader, and he kept everybody in tow.

Finally, though playing under a rookie coach like Jean Perron had required some serious adjustments and not everyone had flourished, when all was said and done, Jean had led us to a Stanley Cup in his rookie season. Only a handful of guys can make that claim.

CHAPTER 18

The Long Goodbye

"If anything, I don't want to be known as a great player. I want to be known as a great teammate." – LARRY ROBINSON (quoted in "Habs Heroes" by Ken Campbell of *The Hockey News*)

We had a good season defending our Stanley Cup in 1986–87, finishing second to Hartford in the Adams Division. We found a new gear in the playoffs while blanking the Bruins in the first round, and then—in what was seeming like an annual rite of passage—we faced the Nordiques in the second round. It was the fourth time we'd met each other in the postseason in six years.

The Nordiques won the first two games in the Forum, and we returned the favour by winning the next two games in Quebec City. Game Four was decided on an overtime goal by Mats Näslund and featured an on-ice fight before the opening faceoff had even taken place.

We were tied at two in Game Five when the Nordiques scored a goal that was waved off because of a penalty call against them. Their coach, Michel Bergeron, went ballistic, but it didn't change the call. We came back and scored shortly afterwards, and that was the deciding goal, giving us a three-games-to-two lead in the series. A Quebec City lawyer was prepared to take the game to court, but the Nordiques declined his offer. Although Quebec tied the series in the next game, we returned to the Forum for the seventh game, which we won, 5–3, with all five of our goals were scored in a very productive second period.

We were feeling quite confident about our chances for another Stanley Cup celebration, but our next opponent, the Philadelphia Flyers, beat us in overtime in the opening game. We rebounded in the second game to pull out a solid victory. They won the next two games to go up three games to one, but with the old cliché of our backs against the wall in Game Five, we were strong and once again pulled out a decisive win.

Passions rise to the surface during all hockey games, but during tough playoff series, they seem to instigate all sorts of anger. There is no love, only competitiveness that often takes on vicious overtones. That was certainly the case before the start of Game Six in our conference final series against the Flyers.

Each player has his own rituals and superstitions. Claude Lemieux, for one, liked to wait until the other team had left the ice, and then he'd shoot a puck into the opposing team's net at the conclusion of the pre-game skate. But after word spilled out about Claude's tradition, Philadelphia defenceman Ed Hospodar and goalie Chico Resch attempted to outwait Lemieux and Shayne Corson following the warmup prior to Game Six in Montreal. Lemieux and Corson stepped off the ice just long enough for the Flyers to think they could safely retreat to their dressing room, but as soon as they did,

Claude and Shayne stepped back onto the ice. Hospodar and Resch saw what was happening and scrambled back themselves. Trying to prevent Lemieux and Corson from putting the puck in the Flyer goal, Hospodar slashed Corson and then grabbed Lemieux and started punching. Chico tried to prevent Corson from defending his teammate. The word got back to us in the dressing room that there was a fight on the ice, so we all dashed out, some of us not fully dressed. None of the officials was on the ice, and the scrap quickly escalated, with several fights taking place simultaneously—including one between Chris Nilan and Philadelphia's Dave Brown, who wasn't wearing his sweater or shoulder pads.

We all were milling about, guys taking swipes when they had the chance, and someone sucker-punched me. I was later told it was Don Nachbaur. The brawl went on for quite a while before the officials settled things down and got both teams to their dressing rooms. When the game finally began, the Montreal fans booed "The Star-Spangled Banner." We scored quickly, but Philadelphia went on to win 4–3, earning a trip to the Stanley Cup final against the Edmonton Oilers.

There were a lot of these ridiculous brawls in the 1970s and '80s. They were a blight on the game and posed real potential for someone to get hurt, and the NHL was wise to institute the third-man-in rule and to fine and penalize players who leave the bench to fight.

•

Though we were disappointed to miss out on the Stanley Cup final in 1987, the 1987–88 season was especially frustrating, both personally and professionally. I suffered a broken leg playing polo the previous summer and wasn't able to get back into action until late November. People questioned whether my career was over, but I worked out very hard to return—*very* hard. I reported to training camp three weeks early, only a few weeks after the operation on my broken leg, since I had a lot of work to do to bring it back to full strength and mobility.

The first week, I rode the bike and did some light exercises with Gaétan Lefebvre, the physiotherapist for the Canadiens, and built up my routine as the weeks went on. By the time my teammates reported for camp, I was feeling really good, but I hadn't yet tried to skate. I knew the media would be all over my first attempt, so we rented some ice in Dollard-des-Ormeaux and I gingerly stepped onto the rink that morning at 6:30. I skated with Gaétan and my friend, Donny Cape, for about half an hour, and the leg felt pretty good. I even shot a few pucks. The next day, I did the same thing, but I stayed on the ice for an hour that time. It was the same for the next few days, and each time I'd work the leg a little harder, skating hard forward and backwards and then trying to make quick turns. Soon the leg felt ready, and I wasn't nervous about joining my teammates for practice at the Forum with the media guys looking on. Having said that, it was almost Christmas before I finally felt like I was at 100 per cent again.

We finished first in the Adams Division, again collecting more than 100 points, with six guys scoring 20 or more goals. Patrick Roy and Brian Hayward were great in goal for us, winning the Jennings Trophy for the best team goals-against average.

Our first-round opponents in the 1988 playoffs were the Hartford Whalers. We quickly went up three games to none, and maybe subconsciously we figured we were shoo-ins for the series win—but as I learned on the farm, you can never count your chickens before they've hatched. The Whalers gave us quite a scare, winning the next two games before we finally notched that fourth win for the series victory.

Up next were the Bruins, whom we had beaten in the first round four years in a row, sweeping them in three of those years. But we were the two best teams in the Wales Conference this season, and two of the NHL's better defensive teams.

We dropped them 5–1 in the first game, and that was as good as it got for us. The Bruins came back and won the next four to put us out. The record books showed that it was the first time Boston had won a playoff series against the Canadiens in 44 years!

•

You often think about when it might be the right time to leave the game, but I figured that if I had to keep asking myself the question, I wasn't ready to call it quits. I had talked to a number of retired players, and to a man, they all told me the same thing: play as long as you can and don't get out until you have to.

That summer, Serge let Jean Perron go and decided to take a chance on a former police officer who had enjoyed some success at the junior level. That guy was Pat Burns.

Burnsie came in all full of piss and vinegar. He had a reputation as a tough guy to play for, but little did we know that the tough-guy image was a bit of a facade. In Dick Irvin's *Habs*, Burns admitted, "The first time I walked into the dressing room as the coach, I was shaking. I used to watch them play at the Forum sitting in the cheap seats. Now, here I was, coaching the team."

We had a pretty young team, and Bob Gainey and I were, of course, the elder statesmen. In fact, I was a year older than Pat Burns! I had joined the Habs in 1972–73 and Bo had come along a year after me. Actually, Bo had also considered retiring that summer, and had even met with the Minnesota North Stars to discuss their vacant general manager's position, but in the end, he also decided to stay for at least one more season.

Pat realized that Bob and I could lend a great deal to a young team. "They're what it means now to be a Canadien," he said. "They have that tattooed on their hearts, and they make the young guys feel that way, too." Bo and I would often be invited to sit with Pat in his office and talk about our ideas. As two of the leaders on the club, I really thought that was important, and so did Pat.

Bob and I didn't look at the game in the same way we did as kids, but I like to think we went out and tried to play the same way we once did. You can let the game make you old, or you can let it keep you young.

Burnsie tried to alter the system that had been installed under Jean Perron into a more disciplined approach, and it tightened us up defensively. But by asserting himself on the team, Burns created friction. For example, he banned beer on the team bus, he instituted curfews, and he stopped the card games we played—especially when there was money involved. Early in the season, he brought in a Breathalyzer to show the players how little alcohol it takes to be impaired. "The police don't want to hear your story," he told us. "All that's important to them is you've had too many."

These were all good ideas, and would have been very effective with a junior team, but we were all well-paid professional players and a lot of the guys balked at Pat's strategies. It took a while for guys to realize that changes had to be made. He brought discipline to our club, something that had been lacking in previous years. Pat gave the guys lots of freedom, but if they didn't handle it the right way, he reeled them in. He established that he was the boss.

Pat was a hard guy to read at first. He would scream and yell, swear like a sailor, break his stick over the crossbar of the net—you name it. And yet, there was another Pat: one who would sit in the dressing room, talking and laughing with the guys.

Ten or so games into the season, we were last in our division, and the press was calling for Pat's head. A headline in *La Presse* asked,

"Will He Last Until Christmas?" Burnsie just shrugged. "I'm a guy coming into a difficult situation. I'm a new coach with a new system and new ideas. There has to be an adjustment period. Guys were used to doing whatever they wanted to do. I'm trying to put the discipline back in. It's hard at the start, but it will pay off in the long run."

We weren't yet convinced, though, and we didn't seem to have a direction. Were we a team that stressed defence? Were we an attacking team? I didn't see evidence of either, and I seriously considered quitting.

In early November, we traded John Kordic to Toronto for Russ Courtnall. It was a steal of a deal for us: Kordic was big and strong, and John Brophy, the coach of the Leafs, was looking for toughness, but Kordic had a lot of personal problems. In return, we picked up a skilled and speedy forward.

Russ arrived in the middle of the friction, however. "There were definitely some issues with some of the older players and Pat," he remembered. "When I got there, Larry was threatening to quit the team, he was so unhappy."

Bob and I asked for a meeting with Pat. We gave him our vote of confidence and took it upon ourselves to work towards uniting the team. Before a game against Hartford, Bob and I called a players-only meeting, and it really seemed to pull the team together. Then Pat called his own meeting and talked about the gap between the younger players and the veterans. He told us, "You have to wash your dirty laundry together." That resonated with all of us, and it took time, but we made a commitment to work together and fell into a bit of a groove after that. I don't know that the dissension ever fully went away, but the toughest days were behind us, as we only lost two of the next twenty or so games.

Jacques Laperrière, one of our assistant coaches, helped Pat run practices. We watched a lot of video, too. The Canadiens were always well prepared for each game under Pat and Lappy. Burnsie was usually afraid to give the guys a day off, although during the final weeks, he sent me to Florida for five days to rest up for the playoffs. He brought up a few guys from Sherbrooke to give them a taste of the NHL and the Montreal Canadiens. Even though the team continued to win, we didn't win at the same pace, and it might have cost us the Presidents' Trophy, as Calgary finished two points higher than us. But that wasn't really important to any of us, and we ended up having a terrific season, earning 115 points.

Early in the season, Burns had stated, "I don't want to be coach of the year; I want to be the coach for a year!" After things had settled down, Pat did a nice job and *was* named coach of the year, winning the Jack Adams Award.

Patrick Roy won the Vézina (which was now for the goalie judged to be best at his position), and he and Hayward took the Jennings Trophy again. The First All-Star Team featured Patrick and Chris Chelios, who also won the Norris. It was our defence that excelled in 1988–89.

We defeated the Hartford Whalers, the Bruins, and the Philadelphia Flyers in the playoffs before meeting the Calgary Flames in the Stanley Cup final, a rematch of 1986. We won Game Three in overtime on a goal by Ryan Walter, and I hugged him so hard afterwards that he told reporters he was numb! But after a go-ahead goal from Lanny McDonald, Calgary took the Stanley Cup in Game Six at the Montreal Forum, the only time that a visiting team had ever beaten the Canadiens to win the Cup on Forum ice.

I thought we were the better team in the final against Calgary, but they earned the right to hoist the Stanley Cup. We were crushed to see them parading it around our rink, but we knew we had given everything we had.

Following the loss, Bob Gainey announced his retirement. And while I didn't realize it at the time, when I pulled off my sweat-soaked jersey after that game on May 25, 1989, it would be the last time I would wear *la sainte-flanelle*—the "holy flannel"—as a member of the Montreal Canadiens.

CHAPTER 19

California Dreaming

"Larry was an idol of mine growing up, I was very fortunate to have great players like Larry in the dressing room to help shape me and guide me as a player." – ROB BLAKE (on NHL.com)

Montreal had been a special home to me from 1973 until 1989. If you're ever going to play in a place that's going to help your career, it's Montreal. They never settled for second-best. Playing there is either going to make you or break you. It broke quite a few guys, but it also made a lot of great hockey players over the years, and I was fortunate enough to be one of them. The people there treated me unbelievably well, and there's no other place I would rather have played.

I became a free agent after the 1988–89 season and decided that I'd play one more season in Montreal. There wasn't a great deal of negotiating: Serge offered me a one-year deal at a million dollars plus a retirement bonus. I really wanted to stay with the Canadiens, but I got the feeling that the club had reached the conclusion that my productive playing career was at an end.

Serge and I were very good friends, having not only been defence partners but roommates with the Canadiens. When Serge retired from playing in 1983 and was hired as general manager of the Canadiens, he told me my number would be retired when my playing days were over. I brought up the subject during our negotiations, but Serge told me that the Canadiens had no immediate plans for such an occasion. I was terribly disappointed, but more unhappy that I wasn't made to feel wanted by a franchise that I loved—and where I had worked incredibly hard to be successful.

Later, I was at Dingy's, discussing my situation with Donny Cape in our office. His was such a great voice of reason. I was telling him that I thought I'd like to play one more year, and we started to discuss possibilities. To be candid, I didn't know if any other team would be interested in a 17-year veteran.

At the time, there was a lot of excitement about hockey in Los Angeles, and we talked about the possibility of playing for the Kings. Bruce McNall had purchased 25 per cent of the franchise in 1986, and then bought the remaining shares from Jerry Buss in 1988. The Kings had been trying to trade for Wayne Gretzky for a number of years, but for McNall it became almost an obsession. He made Peter Pocklington, the Edmonton Oilers' owner, a wild offer in 1988 at the NHL Awards, and a week later, Pocklington called him back and agreed to make the deal—having figured that Gretzky wasn't going to re-sign with the Oilers when his contract expired. Plus, Wayne had just married Janet Jones and was staying in Hollywood in a home owned by Alan Thicke, so Pocklington seemed to believe that a deal with Los Angeles was the right deal at the right time. The money had already been agreed upon, and it was just a matter of which other players were going to be included. The deal was announced on August 9, 1988, while the entire hockey world—in fact, just about the entire continent—looked on.

So L.A. seemed to be on the rise. Plus, my old teammate Rogie Vachon was the GM there. Donny said, "Why don't we call McNall and see what he has to say? You have nothing to lose."

We told Bruce that I'd be interested in talking to him about joining the Kings, and his first response was, "Are you kidding? We're very interested!" He offered to fly me, Donny Cape and our wives to L.A. to look around and see how we felt about the city. What the heck? We had nothing to lose, as Donny had said, so off we went.

Bruce wined and dined us. We discussed details over dinner at Wolfgang Puck's, where Bruce offered me a two-year contract with an option for a third season. "Holy mackerel," I thought. "That's a pretty good deal!" The money was good, but more than that, I started to like the idea of a new start with a team that was really excited about having me.

We called Serge in Montreal right from Bruce's office and offered the Canadiens the opportunity to match the Kings' deal. Serge said, "I'm sorry, Larry, but we can't match your offer from Los Angeles," and wished me well. I was a bit melancholy, as I was leaving a team and a city that I loved, but soon Jeannette and I were moving to California. I signed the deal on July 25, 1989, and two days later, Bruce and I appeared on the short-lived *Pat Sajak Show* on the CBS network to announce that I'd be joining the Kings. Sajak, of course, was the host of *Wheel of Fortune*, and the other guests on his talk show that night were actor Leslie Nielsen, singer Peter Allen, and a comedian named John Riggi.

Little did I know what an exciting year my first season in L.A. would be—the highlight of which was witnessing Wayne Gretzky break Gordie Howe's NHL career scoring record.

Wayne Gretzky idolized Gordie Howe, and had throughout his entire life. Who would have thought, when Wayne was 11 years old and meeting Gordie at a hockey banquet, that one day he'd beat Howe's NHL scoring record?

Gordie had collected 1,850 points through his phenomenal career. Wayne had 1,849 going into a game on October 15, 1989, which as luck would have it was in Edmonton—the city where he had set so many scoring records and helped win so many Stanley Cups. The significance wasn't lost on any of us.

Wayne tied Howe's record with an assist early in the game. But would he break it? We were down 4–3 in the third with about three minutes to go when Tom Webster, our coach, called a time-out. The Edmonton fans began to cheer: "*Gretz-ky! Gretz-ky! Gretz-ky!*" The sound was deafening. They wanted the record for Wayne as if he was still one of their own.

With about a minute left to go, and with our goalie pulled for an extra attacker, Steve Duchesne kept possession of the puck in the Oilers zone. He fired it to Dave Taylor, who relayed it to Gretz in front of the net. Wayne backhanded the puck over Bill Ranford, who was sprawled in the Edmonton crease, to score his record-breaking 1,851st point. The leading scorer in the history of the National Hockey League—unbelievable!

Wayne was hopping with excitement, and he leapt right into my arms. They stopped the game for an on-ice celebration, and Wayne's wife, Janet, came down with his dad, Walter. Bruce McNall came down as well, as did Wayne's hockey hero himself, Gordie Howe.

Mark Messier presented Wayne with a gold bracelet with diamonds on behalf of the Edmonton Oilers organization. Dave Taylor and I presented Gretz with a crystal hologram on behalf of the Kings. NHL president John Ziegler gave Wayne a sterling silver tea set engraved with the logos of each of the NHL teams.

When play resumed, all Wayne did was go on to score the game-winning goal.

Despite the individual heroics, the team didn't play particularly well that season, and after 17 years with the Canadiens, I found the transition to playing with the Kings more challenging than I imagined. The *Los Angeles Times* suggested that I should have played in the Legends game at the All-Star Weekend.

At first, playing with Gretz was a detriment. I had watched Wayne for a number of years, and played against him as well. When I first went to Los Angeles, I changed my style a little bit, trying to play more offensively, but that was never my strong suit. Finally, I sat down with Rogie. I was struggling and thought I had lost it, but he told me that the Kings didn't sign me to play like Wayne—or to play the style that anybody else was playing. He wanted me to play the style that I had played all my years in Montreal. "We want a steady defenseman who can move the puck," he told me. That really helped me, and it got me turned back in the right direction.

In the first round of the playoffs, we faced the reigning Stanley Cup champion Calgary Flames—those same Flames who had defeated us the previous spring in Montreal—and we eliminated them in six games. Then we found ourselves up against the Oilers, whom the Kings had knocked out of the playoff race the previous year. But Edmonton had our number this time. Esa Tikkanen completely neutralized Gretz—I think he might have held Wayne to a single point. We competed with them in every game, especially in L.A., but they swept us in four games, and then went on to win the Stanley Cup.

We came back strong the next year, finishing first in the Smythe Division in 1990–91 with more than 100 points (the second-best finish in the Kings' history). We beat the Vancouver Canucks in the division semifinals, but once again advanced to face the Edmonton Oilers, and once again, they ended our playoff run.

The 1991–92 season was the option year of my contract with the Kings, and Jeannette and I made the decision that it would, in fact, be my final year. The Kings had a pretty good season, finishing second in our division. And you don't even need to guess whom we faced: the Edmonton Oilers, of course. This was a different Oilers team, though—Mark Messier, Glenn Anderson, and Grant Fuhr were gone—but it didn't matter; the results were the same. We split the first four games, but then Edmonton took control of the series and won the next two to end our season. My final NHL game was a 3–0 loss to Edmonton in Game Six that spring.

•

Playing in Los Angeles was a very enjoyable experience for me, but very different than my time with the Canadiens. A hockey game in Montreal is not a hockey game; it's an outing. The fans are very, very knowledgeable and come to witness a spectacle. The Montreal Forum was just like a palace, and the atmosphere there was next to none. I truly, truly loved playing there. It was just always my favourite place to play. In fact, even when I wore the L.A. Kings uniform, I still loved playing on that ice in the Forum in Montreal. I have to say that the people embraced me and were very, very kind to me, and still are to this day. They're great, great people to play in front of.

Los Angeles was a little different. The fans are very enthusiastic, and though I won't go so far as to say they're not as knowledgeable, it's more of a crowd that goes to be seen. I absolutely loved my experience of playing hockey at the Great Western Forum with the Kings. Los Angeles is also a great place to play, and I have some great memories of playing—and, later, coaching—there. The current crowd at the Staples Centre is a little different than at the Forum because they've really built themselves a tremendous fan base now in L.A.

I never got really close to Bruce McNall, though. He was an extremely nice guy, and I owe him a great deal for bringing me to

Los Angeles, but he and I led completely different lifestyles. I am a very simple guy, a farm boy, and he wasn't really what I'm accustomed to. Being more of a family man, I liked to hang around with Dave Taylor, Tommy Laidlaw, and Timmy Watters. We were kind of the meat-and-potatoes group that hung out together. We were all pretty low-key and did a lot of things together with our kids.

Much has been made of McNall's financial situation and his later jail term, but all I know is that what he did for hockey in California is truly remarkable. Hockey wouldn't be where it is in Los Angeles had it not been for Bruce McNall, and the Kings owe a great deal to him. Good, bad, or indifferent, I don't hold anything against him whatsoever.

Gretz. Wayne Gretzky. Just a great guy. Everything that's been said and written about him is exactly what he is. What he has accomplished is unfathomable: he has every right to be called "The Great One." I only played with Gretz in his later years, but to score more than 90 goals and 200 points in a season is extraordinary. I admire him greatly, and while he wasn't a guy I hung around with in L.A., Wayne was truly a great teammate.

Luc Robitaille is another guy I really, really like. Lucky made the most out of his capabilities. He wasn't the greatest skater in the world, but when I think of pure scorers, I think of Steve Shutt, Mike Bossy, and Luc. When that puck was on their stick, it was in the net. Lucky loved to compete and loved to win. When we were teammates, he was just a terrific person with a big heart who liked a good time and loved to laugh.

I really enjoyed playing with Robbie Blake as well. Right near the end of my career, when Blakey came in, I wanted to take him under my wing because, when I looked at him, I saw myself: tall, rangy, and probably didn't know how good he could really be. But a good skater, with a good shot.

Because I was older and had been in the league longer, there were a lot of things I had learned that I passed on to the younger guys. (Though, at the time, it never even crossed my mind that someday I was going to be a coach.) The mentorship started back in Montreal, when Serge used to pair me with every new kid that came to the team as a defenceman. I wouldn't say that it hurt my career, but a lot of times I was playing on the right side, where I didn't feel as comfortable. I preferred the left side, and that's where I played when I was on the blue line with Serge. But all of a sudden, I'd be playing with someone like Gaston Gingras, and because he played left, I was moved over to the right (being more able to do that). That meant that a lot of times, when the puck came around the boards, I would be on my backhand. I had to reinvent my game and learn to play it from the right side.

The same thing happened when I was in L.A. I played with Brian Benning, I played with Timmy Watters, and then Steve Duchesne came in as a rookie during my last big playoff series and I was teamed with him most of the time. That was actually a good pairing for us, especially since he liked to play the right side.

While I was passing along little tricks to the young defencemen, there was a lot of stuff they taught me, too. I think Gordie Howe said it the best: he played until he was 52, and the reason he did was because you never stop learning. You either learn something about yourself or you learn something about the game. You're always learning new tricks and new ways to do things. You're always striving to make yourself better.

That is the biggest thing that I try to get across to all the guys that I'm coaching now. Mistakes are part of hockey, and if you don't communicate with your partner and you're not talking on the ice, then it just makes it so much harder for you. You're a tandem. That's why they call it a hockey *team*. It's not a hockey individual; it's a hockey *team*. You have to work together.

CHAPTER 20

International Man in History

"Larry Robinson was so big, so mobile, and especially, so strong. He was overly polite, and that drove me crazy. Here was a guy you couldn't get mad at. He was just massive, and strong. You couldn't get around him." – BRYAN TROTTIER

The Summit Series of 1972 had pitted the world's two hockey superpowers—Canada and the Soviet Union—in a tournament that, for the first time, saw both countries able to use their best players. Previous to that series, international competitions had been restricted to amateurs only, but the success of the Summit Series would encourage organizers to plan additional international tournaments.

However, in 1972, there was great controversy because only NHL players were invited to play in the Summit Series, meaning that guys who had jumped to the WHA were not allowed to play for a Team Canada squad that was intended to showcase the country's best players. That meant that guys like Gerry Cheevers, Bobby

Hull, Derek Sanderson, and J.C. Tremblay, who would all likely have made the team had they still been committed to play in the NHL, were excluded.

Another series between the Soviet Union and Canada was held in 1974, but this time, it was only WHA players who were allowed to play. While Canada had won the Summit Series in 1972 with four wins, three losses, and a tie, in 1974 it was the Soviets who were victorious with four wins, one loss, and three ties.

There was a genuine fascination with playing the Soviets that was derived from that 1972 Summit Series. The simple game of hockey was escalated in stature so that the outcome would not only establish hockey dominance but serve as a verdict on which way of life was superior: freedom and democracy versus communism.

In late 1975 and early 1976, CSKA Moscow (also known as the Central Red Army) and the Soviet Wings travelled to North America for four games each against NHL teams in what was billed as the Super Series. Our game in Montreal, the second of four that the Red Army would play, was scheduled for New Year's Eve at the Forum.

Scotty prepared us well. Even though it was an exhibition game, we knew that there was much more on the line than that. The eyes of the hockey world were on us. Could we contain the speed and finesse of the Soviets? Could we beat the amazing Vladislav Tretiak? Could they compete against the creativity of our offence and our suffocating defence?

What transpired has been called "the greatest hockey game ever played."

Before the opening faceoff, I was standing on the blue line while the anthems were being sung, knowing that millions of people were going to see the game. It was frightening, to say the least. But it was also a terrific feeling.

After the puck dropped, Steve Shutt and Yvon Lambert scored

on Tretiak before the game was eight minutes old. The Soviets, while very good, didn't look like Supermen, as we had been led to expect. They didn't get their first shot on Kenny until ten minutes into the game, and they only got four shots all period.

Meanwhile, how good was Tretiak? That tall standup stance wasn't a great deal different than Dryden's. And Tretiak was good. Damned good. He forced you to make the first move. He would just stare down the shooters. He robbed Coco late in the first period with a sensational save.

Still, Cournoyer added to our lead in the second period. We were again strong defensively and only surrendered three shots the entire period. But they didn't need many more—two of them went into our net.

The only goal scored in the third period was by the Soviets, and it tied the game. It was one of only six shots the Red Army got in the third. Again, Tretiak stoned Lemaire, this time late in the game, with the victory on the line.

We outshot the Soviets 38–13, and yet the game ended in a 3–3 tie. The Red Army Club capitalized on its scoring chances, in spite of the fact we played a great defensive game. Even Scotty, who hated any game that didn't result in a Montreal win, was smiling. He knew we were the better team, and if not for the brilliance of Tretiak, we'd have skated away with the victory. "This team was ready," he told reporters. "This team did everything it had to do. We should have won, and that's a little disappointing, but I'm proud of this team."

The Red Army ended up winning two, tying one, and losing one in their trip to North America. The Soviet Wings finished with three wins and a loss.

Today, that contest is regarded as legendary. There was so much emotion, so much pressure, and so much pride. I didn't mind giving up my New Year's Eve for what now is considered a historic game.

•

There were more high-profile matchups to come. In 1976, Alan Eagleson, who was the executive director of the National Hockey League Players' Association, and Douglas Fisher, head of Hockey Canada, worked together with hockey officials in the Soviet Union to plan for a new tournament that they would call the Canada Cup. Like the Summit Series, it would be played in September, just before the NHL season was to begin. Organizers invited six countries to take part in the inaugural tournament: Canada, Czechoslovakia, Finland, the Soviet Union, Sweden, and the United States.

Sam Pollock was chosen to put Team Canada together, and he asked Scotty Bowman to coach the team. Scotty was still coaching the Canadiens, and we had just won the Stanley Cup that spring. As assistant coaches, Sam and Scotty chose Don Cherry, who was coaching the Bruins; Bobby Kromm, who had just coached the Winnipeg Jets to the WHA championship; and my old coach, Al MacNeil, who had coached the Voyageurs to the AHL championship.

The management group invited a strong field of player candidates from across the NHL and the WHA, and we met at the Queen Elizabeth Hotel in Montreal. There were some sensitivities that went back to 1972, when a handful of players invited to play in the Summit Series were disappointed by their lack of ice time and returned to their NHL training camps after the first four games of the series. We were reminded that we were all there to play for Canada.

There was a lot of great talent at that training camp, and there were difficult choices for the coaching staff to make. Phil Esposito was one of the first guys to speak up and tell us that we had to stick together as a team and not let our individual egos get in the way—but towards the end, they were thinking of cutting Phil, and all of a sudden he had to put his body where his mouth was. They decided to keep him, and he was a huge contributor to our team. It wasn't just Phil who was on thin ice, though: I was also a candidate to be cut near the end. It was between me and Paul Shmyr, who was playing for the Cleveland Crusaders of the WHA, and I was fortunate to end up being the one to stay.

Kenny Dryden was hurt at the time, so the goalies they picked were Gerry Cheevers, Glenn Resch, and Rogie Vachon. On defence, there were Guy Lapointe, Bobby Orr, Denis Potvin, Serge Savard, Carol Vadnais, Jimmy Watson, and me. Shmyr was kept on as a reserve. The forwards selected were Bill Barber, Bobby Clarke, Marcel Dionne, Phil Esposito, Bob Gainey, Danny Gare, Bobby Hull, Guy Lafleur, Reggie Leach, Peter Mahovlich, Richard Martin, Lanny McDonald, Gilbert Perreault, Steve Shutt, and Darryl Sittler. Jean Pronovost and René Robert were reserves. Because Pronovost was more senior, he got my number 19 and I wore 23. Didn't matter to me.

My boyhood idol had been Bobby Hull, and all of a sudden, he was my roommate (although I barely saw him in the room for the whole tournament). On the ice, I was partnered on defence with Bobby Orr. Bobby had considered declining the invitation because his knee was really bothering him, and since the tournament was the world's best playing against the world's best, he didn't want to be playing at half speed. But after a couple of workouts, he knew that the chance to play for his country was something he couldn't pass up.

We knew we had a very strong team, and the Soviets were always exceptionally good, but we didn't really know how good the other four teams were going to be. The Czechs were certainly no slouches at the time: just a few months earlier, they had earned a silver medal at the Winter Olympics, and they had also won the gold medal at the World Championship. I remember the Czech coach stating that he wanted to prove to the world that there was more to international hockey than Canada and the Soviet Union.

The series began with a five-game round robin, and anything can happen in a short series, but Team Canada played extremely well. We finished in first place with our only loss a frustrating 1–0 shutout against the Czechs. In fact, while most believed that, once again, the final would see Canada face the Soviet Union, Czechoslovakia surprised everyone and earned a spot in the best-of-three Canada Cup final.

Game One took place in Toronto at Maple Leaf Gardens. We scored four goals in the first period on Vladimir Dzurilla, the Czechoslovak goalie, and they replaced him in net with Jiri Holeček, who played pretty well but still gave up two more goals. Vachon was sensational in net for us, and Canada waltzed to a convincing 6–0 victory.

Game Two was played on September 15 at the Montreal Forum, and was an entirely different game. Holeček started in goal this time for the Czechs, but after Canada scored twice in the first three minutes, he was replaced by Dzurilla.

Czechoslovakia was much stronger for the rest of the game, tying the score early in the third and then taking a lead. With just over two minutes left in the game, the Czechs were up 4–3, but Bill Barber scored to tie the contest and send it into sudden-death overtime. The action was fast and furious, as both teams badly wanted to win the Canada Cup. Dzurilla and Vachon were equally amazing in their respective goals. Guy Lafleur looked to have scored the winner when his shot snuck past the Czechoslovakian netminder, but the net was knocked out of place just as the puck crossed the goal line—and while the Czech player responsible was given a delay of game penalty, his action prevented our victory. Later, Guy Lapointe beat Dzurilla, but the goal was again waved off as the buzzer had sounded to end the first 10 minutes of the overtime period. International rules called for play to be stopped at the 10-minute mark of any overtime period in order for teams to switch ends.

Don Cherry had been watching the game from the stands, and he came down to give us some advice on Dzurilla. He had noticed that the goalie had a habit of coming way out of his net to cut down the angle on shooters. Cherry told us that, if we got the chance, we should fake, get him out of position, and then go by him. Sure enough, just a minute later, Marcel Dionne fed a great pass to Darryl Sittler on the left boards. Sittler broke down his wing, but as he approached the Czech goal, Dzurilla came way out to challenge him. Using Cherry's advice, Darryl faked a slapshot and then took an extra stride. Dzurilla was out of position and Darryl had a wide-open net in which to score the winning goal.

There was a great celebration, not only with the players on the ice, but by the fans in the stands of the Montreal Forum as well. Pete Mahovlich had a great idea, and in a sign of goodwill, we exchanged jerseys with the Czech players. Pierre Trudeau presented the newly minted Canada Cup to Bobby Clarke, our captain. The trophy was too heavy to carry, so we left it on the table where it had been presented and simply took a victory lap around the Forum ice, waving and wearing the jerseys of our opponents.

Rogie Vachon was awarded a new car as Team Canada's MVP. Bobby Orr was phenomenal in what would prove to be the last hurrah of his extraordinary career and was presented with the tournament's Most Valuable Player award.

That may very well be the best team I ever played on. Sixteen members of that team are now Honoured Members of the Hockey Hall of Fame, along with our coach, Scotty Bowman. There were no egos. It didn't matter what province you came from or what your politics were; we were all simply Canadians, and it was an honour to have been part of something that brought people together like that. It was quite memorable for me.

•

A touring Soviet team became a fairly regular occurrence, and we found ourselves playing Moscow Spartak on January 6, 1978. We beat them 5–2, one of only two losses they suffered during their five-game exhibition series against NHL teams in North America.

Later that year, during the 1978–79 season, the NHL decided to replace the usual All-Star Game with a three-game Challenge Cup series between a team of NHL All-Stars and one from the Soviet Union. All three games took place at Madison Square Garden in New York City.

Balloting selected the starting lineup, and I was proud to be chosen to start on defence along with Denis Potvin. The forwards voted in were Bobby Clarke, Guy Lafleur, and Steve Shutt. Tony Esposito was the goalie chosen, although he did not play, and instead Scotty Bowman, with help from Claude Ruel, selected Ken Dryden and Gerry Cheevers. They added Barry Beck, Guy Lapointe, Börje Salming, and Serge Savard to the blue line, and at forward, the team included Billy Barber, Mike Bossy, Marcel Dionne, Bob Gainey, Clark Gillies, Anders Hedberg, Don Marcotte, Lanny McDonald, Kent Nilsson, Gilbert Perreault, Darryl Sittler, and Bryan Trottier. Ron Greschner and Robert Picard were spares.

The Soviet team had been playing together since July, but even though many of us had never played together, with our stacked lineup, we believed we could do well against the USSR.

We faced our old nemesis Vladislav Tretiak in goal for the Soviets in Game One, and it looked like we had him and the Soviets figured out when Flower scored 16 seconds into the game. We went on to win the first game 4–2. Tretiak was shaky in Game Two, allowing a couple of soft goals, and early in the second, we were up 4–2.

That changed pretty quickly, as the Soviets found a new gear, battled back hard, and ended up edging us 5–4.

The final game was a disaster. We had learned from previous series that the Soviets didn't like to be hit, so we tried to lay the body on them, but that tactic certainly didn't work in this series. The Soviets also replaced Tretiak with a rookie goaltender, Vladimir Myshkin, and he was sensational. The first period was scoreless, and after two, the Soviets were up 2–0. We just couldn't get anything going, and they skated us into the ice. The final score was a humiliating 6–0.

The Challenge Cup in 1979 made us aware that Canada was no longer the dominant hockey force in the world. It was our game, true, but other countries had adopted it and made it their own. While in the scheme of things, this exhibition series was meaningless, it made us realize that, as a country, we needed to adapt our game if we had hopes of continuing to dominate.

•

Fans regarded that game on New Year's Eve 1975 as a hockey classic, and all concerned hoped to capture lightning in a bottle once again by arranging another Super Series in 1979. The Canadiens were four-time Stanley Cup champions, and while we had lost Dryden, Cournoyer, and Lemaire (and Scotty had moved on), we still had a formidable team. On New Year's Eve 1979, the Canadiens again faced the Red Army in what everyone hoped would be a game as thrilling as the one in '75.

Not even close.

Things were especially bad for me: on my first shift, I got cross-checked and ended up with cracked ribs. It hurt to breathe, but I kept playing. Later on, I shifted to avoid a check and fell, and in doing so, I sprained my wrist.

Going into the third period, the Soviets were up 2–1, but as we did so often, we stormed back in the third with three goals, two by Steve Shutt, to win the game 4–2. The only similarity to the 1975 clash was the way we dominated the Red Army in shots. This time, we outshot them something like 35–14. Viktor Tikhonov, coach of the Red Army team, said, "It's the best team we played." But Red Army played five games against NHL teams in this series, winning three.

•

A few years later, in the spring of 1981, the Canadiens had enjoyed an incredible end-of-season run, losing just once in our last 27 games. But, just our luck, that was the year we faced the Edmonton Oilers in the opening round and were swept in three games straight. Our triumphant and hopeful season came to a very sudden conclusion.

But the Flower and I were selected to join the Canadian team at the World Championship, which was to take place in Sweden. Eight teams, divided into two groups, took part, with Canada's group including Finland, the Netherlands, and the Soviet Union.

This was a new experience for us, as the team was made up of the better players from teams that didn't make the playoffs, plus a few guys whose teams had been eliminated early from playoff competition. Don Cherry, who had been away from coaching for a year, was behind the bench for Team Canada. Our goalies were John Garrett and Phil Myre, and on the blue line we had Dave Babych, Norm Barnes, Rick Green, Willie Huber, Barry Long, Rob Ramage, and me. Our forwards were Pat Boutette, Lucien DeBlois, Mike Foligno, Mike Gartner, Morris Lukowich, Dennis Maruk, Dale McCourt, Lanny McDonald, John Ogrodnick, Mike Rogers, Steve Tambellini, and Ryan Walter.

This whole experience was a friggin' nightmare! It was all so quick that I barely stopped: Guy and I left Edmonton after our final game on April 11 and flew overnight to Montreal, where we got our clothes and our equipment. Jeannette and I might have said two words before we left that morning for Toronto, and then flew from Toronto to Sweden. We got into Sweden around four o'clock on the afternoon of April 13.

John Ferguson, who was the GM, asked us if we wanted to play against the Netherlands in the first game, which took place the evening of our arrival. He said it'd be good us to get used to the Olympic-sized ice. We said we would. Then, on his first shift, Flower reached back to take a pass and was elbowed by this Junior B kid—and got knocked out. I laughed, "Flower! No fair! You're getting a rest and I can't!" Guy couldn't remember anything. He lost his memory for a whole day, plus he was cut for a few stitches across the bridge of his nose. If there was any vengeance, we ended up beating them 8–1.

Getting that game under my belt was a pretty good experience, though. European hockey, with its big ice surfaces, is a whole different game. I was a physical player, so the first time I went to bodycheck a guy in the corner, I looked back and could only think, "Holy mackerel! That's a long way to go back to the front of the net!" You had to change your game a lot.

But my biggest problem occurred off the ice, where I did something stupid. I was fooling around with those wooden Q-Tips in my ears, pretending I was a Martian to make my teammates laugh, and ended up popping an eardrum. Talk about pain! Oh my God. It was like somebody shot a gun off in my head! Guy was my roommate in Sweden, and he gagged when I would get up in the morning, because my pillow would be full of blood and this oozing stuff that was coming out of my ear. That went on for two or three days, and when my ear finally started to come around a little bit, they put a bit of a patch in it. I had a constant whistle and I couldn't hear out of my left ear: when I was playing, if my partner was calling for the puck, I had to look first. I had no sense of direction, and played the whole tournament with one ear.

We finished second to the Soviets in our group, but the top two teams advanced to the final stage. We just couldn't compete, however, and finished fourth out of the four teams that reached the final round. The Soviet Union took gold, and Don Cherry called them "the best Russian team I've ever seen."

Tretiak of the Soviet Union was named Best Goalkeeper and Alexander Maltsev was Best Forward. I was very proud to be named Best Defenceman, but all in all, it was a very strange tournament for me, and one that, for the most part, I'd prefer to forget.

•

The second Canada Cup took place in September 1981. It was originally planned for 1979, but squabbles among the organizers (and then the Soviet invasion of Afghanistan) delayed it.

The same six teams from the inaugural Canada Cup played in '81: Canada, Czechoslovakia, Finland, the Soviet Union, Sweden, and the United States. Scotty was again chosen to coach our team, and as assistant coaches they added Al MacNeil, who was coaching the Calgary Flames; Pierre Pagé, who was an assistant coach in Calgary; and Red Berenson, the St. Louis Blues' coach. Red really helped me in the tournament, and beyond. He gave me extra attention and helped in different aspects of my game, mostly my skating. I was very appreciative. He had a positive effect on my career.

We went into the tournament with a young team. Both Bobby Orr and Bobby Hull had retired by this point. And though Wayne

Gretzky was only 20, he had won the scoring title the previous season. There was Mike Bossy from the Stanley Cup champion New York Islanders, who was my roommate and a guy I really liked, along with his teammates Bryan Trottier, Clark Gillies, Butch Goring, Denis Potvin (who was named captain), and Billy Smith in goal—although he was injured. Guy Lafleur was also back, playing with Gretzky and Gilbert Perreault on our top line. We also had Marcel Dionne, Ron Duguay, Bob Gainey, Danny Gare, Ken Linseman, and Rick Middleton. On defence, there was Barry Beck, Ray Bourque, Craig Hartsburg, Brian Engblom, and Paul Reinhart, and Mike Liut was in goal, with Don Edwards backing him up. Bill Barber, Steve Shutt, and Darryl Sittler were among those invited to training camp, but they were later cut. I know each was disappointed, but not bitter.

The press pegged us as the team to beat, but warned that the Soviets had rebuilt nicely and would provide stiff competition. They were right!

The tournament format had been changed for 1981. There was still the five-game round robin, but a semifinal was added, followed by a single-game championship final. We breezed through the round robin, winning four and tying the Czechs. The Soviets finished behind us in second. After the semi, it was, as predicted, Canada versus the Soviet Union.

Both coaches prepared their teams as though it was war. Scotty insisted that it was a must-win game, saying, "Nobody in this country will tolerate a loss." Meanwhile, the Soviet coach, Viktor Tikhonov, told his team, "You must play so well that the entire Canadian population will talk about you afterwards and remember you for a long time."

The game was played at the Montreal Forum on September 13. We dominated the Soviets in the first period, but simply couldn't beat Tretiak, and the game remained scoreless after one. But then the floodgates burst open, especially for the Soviets, who led 3–1 after the second period. We couldn't get anything going in the third, only mustering a few shots while the Soviets manhandled us. We suffered an embarrassing 8–1 loss.

In spite of the fact that we finished the tournament with four of the top five scorers, it had come down to goaltending in the final game, and Tretiak beat us. He was deservingly named the Most Valuable Player.

As most of the guys were heading home, we learned that there was a luncheon being hosted by Prime Minister Pierre Trudeau for the team. Most guys had travel plans and couldn't go, and as it turned out, only Gretz, Butch Goring, and I went. It was embarrassing: there was the prime minister of Canada and the three of us sitting at a table for 30. Although attendance was sparse, we had a lot of fun with the prime minister, who turned out to be a big fan of the Habs.

Funny story about the actual Canada Cup trophy. The original trophy was made of nickel and weighed about 120 pounds (which is why we left it on the table after winning the previous tournament). It may have been beautiful, but it was impractical, so a lighter replica was made in time for the 1981 tournament. Either way, the trophy wasn't supposed to leave the country, and after they won the series, the Soviet team tried to smuggle the trophy to the Soviet Union in an equipment bag—but Alan Eagleson, accompanied by Montreal police officers, met the Soviet team at the airport and stopped them from taking the Cup. The Soviets disagreed and were quite upset. Finally, a trucker from Winnipeg led a fundraising campaign and had a replica trophy created, which was presented to Soviet officials at their embassy in Ottawa.

•

Because the New Year's Eve game in 1975 was regarded so highly, we were regularly lined up to play a Soviet team on December 31. It was no different in 1982. This time, the Canadiens played the Soviet All-Stars. We usually outshot the Soviet teams so badly, but this time, the shot count was much closer. The score wasn't. The game ended in a 5–0 victory for the All-Stars, with Tretiak once again the star of this less-than-classic contest.

•

Two years later, I was privileged to be invited to again play for Team Canada at the 1984 Canada Cup tournament. As I looked around the dressing room, I realized that I was the old man. In fact, I was the only one who had played in all three Canada Cups.

This time, the Edmonton Oilers' Glen Sather was appointed the coach of Team Canada, and he brought along his Oiler assistants Ted Green and John Muckler. Tom Watt, who had been coaching the Winnipeg Jets, was also an assistant coach.

The team was heavy with Oilers and Islanders, the two teams that dominated the NHL in the 1980s. Glenn Anderson, Paul Coffey, Grant Fuhr, Randy Gregg, Gretz, Charlie Huddy, Kevin Lowe, and Mark Messier were all on the team from Edmonton; and from the Islanders, there was Mike Bossy, Bob Bourne, Brent Sutter, and John Tonelli. Also on the team were Brian Bellows, Ray Bourque, Mike Gartner, Michel Goulet, Rick Middleton, Peter Stastny (who had just become a Canadian citizen), Dougie Wilson, and Steve Yzerman. Besides Fuhr, we had Reggie Lemelin and Pete Peeters as our goaltenders.

This one started with some challenges in the dressing room. Because the team was made up mostly of Oilers and Islanders, there were two distinct factions, and the teams had just faced each other in the Stanley Cup final for a second straight spring. There was absolutely no love lost between them.

Everybody expected that, in order to keep peace, co-captains would be named: one from Edmonton and one from the Islanders—probably Gretz and Bossy. Well, they did name co-captains, but one was Wayne and the other one was me. I was very pleased to be given that honour.

There was still a lot of tension in the room, and as one of the leaders, I did what I could to keep all the guys as unified as possible. If you're not out there having fun, then I don't believe that you're going to have long-term success. We were getting ready for one of our first games and nobody was talking. Around that time, the movie *Flashdance*, starring Jennifer Beals, was out, and its theme song ("Flashdance: What a Feeling" by Irene Cara) came on. My mind works in strange ways sometimes. To break the tension, I started dancing to the song with nothing on but my jockstrap. I went flying from one end of the room to the other, doing my best Jennifer Beals impression. The guys were crying, they were laughing so hard. It was a thing that I did just to loosen everybody up—and then we went out and won the game. Athletes are all superstitious, so naturally, I had to do it each game. It became a ritual, and the joke of that whole Canada Cup.

The split in the team was still causing problems on the ice, however. Some of the New York players thought that, since Glen Sather and the coaching staff were from Edmonton, the Oilers were getting preferential treatment—more ice time, more visibility on the power play. Mike Bossy butted heads with Sather, and while I don't feel he meant it as a shot at Slats, he said things would be different if Al Arbour, the Islanders coach, were behind our bench. Of course they would—they were very different types of coaches—but the media had a field day with the comment anyway.

Though we had beaten West Germany (who had replaced Finland thanks to a strong finish at the World Championships in 1983), we tied the U.S. and then lost to Sweden. We were on the verge of being eliminated from medal contention, and had an important game against the Czechs, but our toughest competition was in our own dressing room.

I don't really look at myself as a vocal leader. I try to lead by example. But I realized that, as one of the senior guys, a captain—and a member of neither the Oilers nor the Islanders—I had to step up. What I tried to get across is that, in order to play well together, you have to get along.

We called a team meeting at Yosemite Sam's, a popular bar in Calgary, and we talked about our differences. I stood up, summoned all my strength, and laid it on the line with the guys. As I went around the room, pointing fingers at every single one of them, I said, "This isn't Team Edmonton Oilers. This isn't Team New York Islanders. This isn't Team Montreal Canadiens. This is Team *Canada*. This bullshit has got to stop!" I knew that if the infighting didn't end and if we didn't play as a team, we'd not only be letting down ourselves down, but our country—and all that fans would remember about the 1984 version of Team Canada was that we choked.

Wayne Gretzky said, "We were all in shock because Larry never did that. And when he made that incredible speech, everyone sort of went, 'Whoa!'" Paul Coffey, who was my defence partner in that tournament, has said that he'll never forget it. "Larry Robinson stood up with as much feeling as I've ever seen a hockey player have."

I think we all believe that the team came together in the next game, which we played in Vancouver. We went out and dominated the Czechs. And even though we lost to the Soviets and finished the round robin with an unimpressive two wins, two losses, and a tie, the Czechs and West Germany both had gone winless—so we were just good enough to earn the fourth and final spot in the semifinals.

The semifinals saw the second-place U.S. facing Sweden, who had finished third. We met the Soviet Union, who had gone undefeated in the round robin. We had our work cut out for us.

We dominated the first couple of periods, but as usual the Soviet goalie was great, and after two periods we led only 1–0. Then, in the third, the Soviets scored while I was off serving a penalty. Too anxious to make amends, I instead made a big mistake on the next shift. Sergei Makarov came down on me at the blue line and made a beautiful fake to the outside, which I fell for hook, line, and sinker. As I floundered, he cut back inside and went in alone on Pete Peeters, beating him with a magnificent deke and a backhand into the net. The Soviets were up 2–1, but Dougie Wilson tied things up late in the third period and the game went to overtime.

It looked like the Soviets were going to end the game when two of their forwards broke across our blue line with only Paul Coffey back to defend. But as one of the Soviets went to send a pass to the other, Coff dropped to his knees and beautifully broke up the two-on-one, and then carried the puck in the opposite direction. In the Soviet end, John Tonelli beat a defender to the puck and passed it back to Coffey at the point. Paul skated in to the top of the faceoff circle and fired a shot that was deflected by Mike Bossy and found the back of the net.

We had beaten the Soviets and earned the chance to play Sweden for the Canada Cup! I immediately phoned home and got my son, and then talked to my wife. That was a pretty amazing game.

After coming back to beat the Soviets, our series against Sweden was anticlimactic. We won Game One in Calgary, 5–2. In Game Two, played in Edmonton, we were up with what I thought was an unbeatable 5–1 lead in the first period before Sweden mounted a comeback that fell just short. They had us on our heels, but the final score was 6–5, and once again we had won the Canada Cup.

Though Gretz and I were the captains of that team, we invited Mike Bossy to join us when we accepted the trophy. Wayne was the top scorer in the tournament, and hard-working John Tonelli was selected as the Most Valuable Player.

We had a really good team, and in spite of the early bullshit, this series was a lot of fun. I had played on what I think were better Canada Cup teams, but I don't think any had more fun than that group in 1984. We played hard, but we partied hard, too. It was also a time when I was questioning whether my game was good enough—a turning point as I neared the end of my career. The tournament was a fun time that made me feel a little bit better about myself.

•

Still capitalizing on that fabled New Year's Eve Game of 1975, organizers planned another for the 10th anniversary, pairing the Canadiens once again with the Red Army team. We didn't outshoot them by much this time (24–22), and we certainly didn't outscore them. Quite the opposite. Funny, but no one talks about the New Year's Eve "classic" of 1985, because we lost 6–1, with Sergei Makarov scoring three for Red Army. Fortunately, winning the Stanley Cup later that season erased most Montrealers' memory of this game.

•

I had one final opportunity to play for my country when I was invited to play in the Canada Cup in 1987. It would have been my fourth tournament, and I would have been the only player to participate in all four Canada Cups. But that was the summer I broke my leg playing polo—so, like everyone else in Canada, I watched on TV as Gretzky fed a perfect pass to Mario Lemieux, who put the puck past the Soviet goalie to give us the Canada Cup once again.

•

Winning the Stanley Cup is an incredible feeling: it's something you dream about from the time you're a kid. There's nothing that can match it, but winning the Canada Cup comes close. In the NHL, we get paid very well to do our best for our team and our fans, but when we played exhibition against teams outside North America, we were playing for our country and for the love of the game. When you play for those reasons, and you're playing with and against the best hockey players in the world, it is incredibly satisfying—and the memories are truly unforgettable.

CHAPTER 21

Transition

"A big step in the progression of the team, and in my personal progression, was when Lou Lamoriello hired Jacques Lemaire and Larry Robinson. For a young defenceman to be able to learn from a guy like Larry was a perfect situation I found myself in. He was very knowledgeable about the game, but what stood out even more to me about Larry was just how he loved life and loved the game. That was pretty contagious." – SCOTT NIEDERMAYER

It was time.

I knew it, and my body certainly reminded me. I retired following the 1991–92 season, which was my 20th in the National Hockey League. I had never been on a team that missed the playoffs during my entire NHL career. I had to look up the stats: 1,384 regular-season games with 958 points—at the time, that was the fourth-highest total ever among NHL defencemen. And I played in 227 playoff games, the most of any player to that date.

Personal awards are wonderful, and I got the opportunity to win six Stanley Cup championships, but the statistic I am proudest of is that I am the NHL's career leader in plus/minus with plus-730.

I enjoyed every second of my career. Like every other young boy, I had dreamed of one day playing in the NHL, but I was a big, awkward kid and the chances were seemed remote for a time. I wasn't a junior sensation like so many of the top draft picks, but I had a good work ethic and great teachers, and they helped me put together a career that, even now, I look back at and can barely believe.

I took a year away from the game and worked for the Bridgestone/ Firestone tire company. Through the garage I owned in Montreal with my friend Donny Cape, I'd gotten to know some people in the tire business. They hired me to be a spokesperson for the company, and I travelled all across Canada, visiting dealerships and garages, doing autograph signings and things like that. That was a fun year, and I travelled from one side of Canada to the other.

There was one promotion in particular where I hosted the top salespeople from each of their dealerships at an all-expenses-paid trip to a resort in Cancún. I was able to bring Jeannette with me, and I have to tell you, it was the most fun we ever had. Just the nicest group of people you could ever imagine. We did all kinds of things during the time in Mexico: golf days, electric car races, and each night, we'd have dinner with a different group of people.

I didn't totally divorce myself from the sport, however. I still watched all the games and played in alumni games. I kept in touch with a bunch of the guys. Hockey never leaves your blood.

•

Then, one day, I got a call at home from Lou Lamoriello, the president and general manager of the New Jersey Devils. I knew of the man, but had never spoken to him before. Lou came right out and asked if I would be interested in being an assistant coach in New Jersey. I had to admit that the thought had never crossed my mind. He told me that he was coming to Montreal and would like to meet with me to discuss the position.

I met Lou at a hotel near the airport, and when I walked in, he was sitting there with Jacques Lemaire. It turned out that Lou had hired Jacques as head coach of the Devils earlier in the week, and when he asked Jacques who he wanted as an assistant coach, Jacques suggested me. When they asked me officially if I would be interested in joining the Devils organization, of course I said yes!

Lou said of me, "The experience and knowledge he will bring to our whole team, and our young defencemen in particular, is invaluable. From the time Jacques mentioned Larry as his first choice for assistant, it became hard to imagine anyone else better suited to our needs."

I was thrilled to be working with Jacques, since we had been friends during our years with the Canadiens. I thought Jean Béliveau nailed it when he stated, "If Ken Dryden was an intellectual, then Jacques Lemaire was a hockey intellectual, but few people realized that until after his playing career was over." Jacques was an outstanding player who really brought the best out in Guy Lafleur, but he was incredibly smart, and no teammate ever studied the game more. He had a great final season as a player, but he was already thinking ahead like a chess game to his next moves.

After he retired in 1979, he'd begun his coaching career with HC Sierre in Switzerland. He was wise to realize that he should get his footing and establish himself as a coach elsewhere before stepping behind the bench of an NHL team. Then he came back to North America as an assistant coach with SUNY Plattsburgh, an NCAA Division III team, and then coached a junior team in Longueil in 1982–83.

While Bob Berry was coaching the Canadiens in 1983–84, Jacques was brought on as an assistant coach. Although he had been quiet as a player and was a great centre for Lafleur, the two butted heads once Jacques was on "the other side," and they had a few loud discussions. Late in the season, Berry was fired and Coco was promoted to head coach. He promptly took us to the Wales Conference final before we lost out to the Islanders. After they brought Jean Perron in to coach, Coco worked with Serge as an assistant to the GM, and was a major contributor to our Stanley Cup wins in 1986 and 1993.

Lemaire really believed that defensive-minded hockey won Stanley Cups, which I agreed with, and he was a great teaching coach, especially with younger players. To be working with Jacques in New Jersey, and being able to work specifically with the defencemen, was an ideal situation for me.

With Jacques's system in place, the Devils enjoyed great success that season. Martin Brodeur, our rookie goalie, was sensational, and he won the Calder Trophy as the league's top first-year player. Scott Stevens led the NHL in plus/minus and was runner-up for the Norris Trophy. We finished in second place, setting team records for wins and points—but more important to me, we cut our goals against by 79 from the year before. Jacques won the Jack Adams Trophy as the NHL's best coach, and we came within a win of going to the Stanley Cup final.

Feeling very positive about our team, we were frustrated by a lockout in 1994–95, which resulted in teams playing only a 48-game season when the issues were resolved. We struggled at the start, but improved substantially as the season went along, and we finished fifth in the Eastern Conference. We were on a roll come playoff time, beating Boston and Pittsburgh in the first two rounds, and then we defeated the Flyers in six games to earn a shot at the Stanley Cup. In the final, we swept the Red Wings to win the championship.

When you win the Stanley Cup as a player, there is great satisfaction. A year of pounding and beatings has come to an end. You've accomplished what you set out to do at the beginning of the season. While you are one part of a larger picture, ultimately, you're responsible for just one person: yourself. But as a coach, it's an entirely different perspective, since you're responsible for a group of players. In my case, as an assistant coach, I was responsible for looking after the defence. I had eight guys that I worked with, and it's a very different feeling. I was flattered when Scott Stevens told *La Presse*, "Larry taught me how to play my position, but he also taught me patience. Teaching is what distinguishes Larry and Jacques Lemaire. They themselves learned from the best. I couldn't imagine how much I had to learn."

As a player, I never got the opportunity to have a day with the Stanley Cup, which all the players, coaches, and trainers get to do these days. So I was thrilled to be able to take the Cup back home to Marvelville for a day in 1995. It was great. My friend Donny and I both had Corvettes—his yellow and mine burgundy. We arrived in Marvelville with the Stanley Cup in our convertibles. We parked right in front of the Marvelville Community Centre, which had been the little one-room school I attended as a boy. Everybody in the area was there. I was so proud that my dad was there to celebrate with us. My grandfather had already passed away, but his brother was there. Uncle Willie was about 104 years old at the time.

Curiously, one of my cousins decided that because I coached in Jersey, he should bring a Jersey cow to the celebration—and he fed the cow out of the Stanley Cup! It was funny, but then I had to disinfect the Cup so that folks could drink beer or champagne out of it.

From there, we stopped in Russell, where I played my minor hockey, and then we made the short trip to nearby Metcalfe, where I went to high school, and took the Stanley Cup to the local arena, which is now named after me. There was a huge turnout, and the place was just packed. Then, we took the Cup to my brother-in-law's restaurant, Tucson's, on Bank Street at Hunt Club in Ottawa. I have to say it was a great day.

Because we've been involved in hockey for a number of years, we sometimes don't appreciate what a thrill it is for people to come up, touch the Cup, and get their picture taken with it. That was the seventh time I had actually held the Cup, but the first time I had it all to myself. It was quite a thrill!

CHAPTER 22

Frustration

"It's real good to win, but it hurts to lose." – LARRY ROBINSON

After the Devils won the Stanley Cup, I got a call from Sam McMaster, who was the Los Angeles Kings' general manager at that time. He asked me if I was interested in taking the head coaching job with his team. Barry Melrose had been let go late in the season, and Rogie Vachon had taken over for the final seven games.

I'd enjoyed my time as an assistant coach, and figured that if I was ever going to try head coaching, this was as good a time as any. I wondered if I'd enjoy the day-to-day pressures of being a head coach, but I'd never know unless I tried it. I accepted the job and signed a four-year contract.

Sam encouraged me to hire my own staff of assistants, so I hired my old teammate Rick Green, along with John Perpich, who was already with the Kings and had previously been with the Washington Capitals. I also hired Don Edwards as our goalie coach.

My first year, we had Wayne Gretzky, but little depth; there was no one in our minor-league system who could step in and help out if we had injuries. There was no base at all. Gretz and I had played together, and I had enormous respect for him. He still had great skills, but we had to look at the big picture. If we wanted to have any kind of a future, trading Wayne was our only way to go. He only had a year left on his contract, and we didn't know whether Gretz was going to retire or sign elsewhere, so we figured it was better to have a little bit of something than be left with nothing. The best offer we got was from St. Louis, and in February 1996, we traded Wayne to the Blues for three guys and a draft pick in 1997—and all four players eventually played for our big club. Wayne had been our captain in Los Angeles, and after the trade, Rob Blake was given the C.

We made a few other trades, too, getting a bit bigger and picking up a few tougher guys. Our goaltending, from Kelly Hrudey and Byron Dafoe, was pretty good as well. We still missed the playoffs, but were building to be a contending team in a year or so. For me, however, that first season with the Kings was disappointing. It was my first-ever time, playing or coaching, that I wasn't part of a playoff team. That was agony.

The next season, 1996–97, Perpich left, and to replace him we hired a guy named Jay Leach, who had been recommended by Jacques Caron, my friend from my days with the Devils' coaching staff. Jay had been with the Hartford Whalers as an assistant coach, and then was a head coach in the AHL. We had so much fun as a coaching staff, and we kept each other standing, but we just didn't have the horses. No matter how I prodded and pushed, I just couldn't turn the team around, and we missed the playoffs again.

There were times when it was difficult for me to coach players who had been my teammates. For example, I had a difficult time dealing with the emotions of guys like Luc Robitaille, Robbie Blake, and Glen Murray because I had played with all three of them on the Kings. One time when we were struggling, those guys came into my office and sat down to talk with me. I shook my head and said, "Guys, I'm stuck. Guys aren't putting out and I don't know what to do." They told me I had to sit players who weren't putting out. I looked at them and said, "The problem is, it's *you* guys who are struggling!" They told me to go ahead and sit them, but I couldn't. "I can't sit you because you're the only ones that are going to win games for us," I admitted. I told them that they had to get themselves out of the doldrums. I wasn't going to win games sitting guys like Luc, Glen, and Blakie. Those were key guys for me.

If I knew then what I know now, I probably should have sat them and suffered for two or three games. It would have sent a pretty strong message to everybody else on the team. But that's one of the things you learn with experience. There are certain decisions you have to make that are going to hurt you in the small picture, but in the big picture are going to pay dividends.

By my third year as coach of the Kings, we had a pretty good, contending team. We increased our points by 20 from the previous season and finished second in the Pacific Division, not far behind Colorado, the best finish for the Kings since their trip to the Stanley Cup final in 1993. We also earned a spot in the playoffs for the first time in five seasons. We were matched with St. Louis in the first round of the playoffs (Gretzky was with the Rangers by then), and while the Blues swept us, three of those games were decided in overtime. I felt a sense of accomplishment with the season, although we still had a long way to go. I was surprised, but pleased, to be named a finalist for the Jack Adams Trophy as coach of the year, and was runner-up to Pat Burns, who had done a terrific job in Boston.

But in 1998–99, we were behind the eight ball from the start. Rob Blake, Luc Robitaille, Jozef Stümpel, and both of our starting goaltenders missed the start of the season with injuries, and we were never able to catch up. Then, halfway through the season, Sam McMaster was fired and replaced by Dave Taylor, who had been a great player for the Kings (part of the Triple Crown Line with Marcel Dionne and Charlie Simmer), but had no managerial experience at all. All of a sudden, I was looking to speak with Dave about issues and he wasn't around: he'd be over in Europe or somewhere, scouting, trying to learn the job as well as trying to find players. Had the Kings done it right, they would have kept Sam, hired Dave, and *then* had Sam help Dave transition into the job. That way, I would have had a little bit of help.

Besides, it was tough losing Sam, who was just a great man with whom I loved working. If I mentioned a player, Sam already knew everything about him. He knew everybody in our minor-league system and made it so much easier for everybody. Dave didn't, because Dave had been a player.

But I knew what that was like. As a player, you step into a managerial job and you have no idea what's going on in the minor leagues or in junior. You have to learn your job as you go along. It put us in a precarious situation, although we got through it and enjoyed it. But after a breakthrough season the year before, we fell back in 1998–99 and finished last in the Pacific.

Furthermore, when Dave Taylor was hired, I sensed my days were numbered as well. We had failed to make the playoffs for three of the four seasons I was with L.A. At the end of that season, I distinctly remember meeting with the ownership group, where they asked if me if I thought they should make trades and get better right away, or stick with the kids. I looked back at the way we did it with the Canadiens: we built strength by bringing the kids along and letting them develop. That's how you get strength in your organization, as I explained to the group. "Listen," I told them, "if you have the patience, we can build this team into a contender."

I left the meeting thinking that that was the strategy we were going to go with, but the next thing I knew, they were trading guys and I was informed that the Kings wouldn't be renewing my contract.

I would never have known what it was like to be a head coach if I hadn't given it a shot. While I certainly tried, I realized it could also be trying. I was disheartened, but little did I know at the time that I was about to get the chance to go home again, in a sense.

CHAPTER 23

A Devil of a Season

"He was one of a kind on the ice and one of a kind off the ice."
– LOU LAMORIELLO

A month after being relieved of my position with the Kings, I was hired by the Devils to return as an assistant coach. I joined Slava Fetisov and goalie coach Jacques Caron to support Robbie Ftorek, the head coach.

One of the main reasons I went back to the Devils was Robbie. He had been L.A.'s head coach a few years before me, but Robbie and I went back to the year of the NHL lockout, 1994–95, when I was an assistant coach with the Devils. During the lockout, Jacques Caron and I were sent down to Albany to work with New Jersey's American Hockey League farm team, the River Rats. Robbie was the head coach there, and he gave me my first taste of what being a coach was all about by letting me organize and run the practices. I ended up going behind the bench with Robbie.

I was in Albany for two months, living in a hotel with Jeannette, and during that time, Robbie and I became really, really good friends. When the lockout ended, I went back to New Jersey, and that season, Albany won the Calder Cup while we won the Stanley Cup. I was really pleased for Robbie—he had done such a great job. And when I went to Los Angeles, Robbie moved up to be an assistant in New Jersey.

So when the opportunity came to return to New Jersey and work with Robbie, who took the head coaching position in 1998–99, I jumped at it. I was not going there to take anybody's job, and I had no ego-driven desire to be the head coach. I just wanted to make Robbie's job easier.

But in March 2000, despite having the best record in the Eastern Conference, the team was in a late-season slump. We had lost 10 of the previous 17 games, and it wasn't a good sign. After having one of the best regular-season records the previous two seasons, we had been embarrassed in the first round of the playoffs both years. Lou did not want that to happen again. With eight games left in the regular season, he decided he had to make a coaching change.

Teams don't change coaches that late in a season very often, but Lou was adamant that the Devils were not going to have a shortened playoff season for a third straight year. Furthermore, hockey should be fun, and it hadn't been recently. Robbie was looked at as a demanding and difficult coach, while I was more of a players' coach. Lou stated, "It had nothing to do with anything personal. This was strictly hockey. In my opinion, for us to have the success, a change was necessary, and Larry was the right person at the right time. It was just what I thought was right."

I got a call from Lou to meet him at the practice rink, where he asked me if I'd take over as head coach. Naturally, my first reaction was, "Holy mackerel! So little time left!" It's always a very difficult situation when you've got to step in for a guy that you're close to. But I chose to take the reins and accepted Lou's offer, while Robbie stayed on in a scouting position.

I had the utmost admiration and respect for Robbie, and appreciated that Robbie had given me a chance to coach during the lockout. But I also knew where some of his shortcomings lay. He treated the stars a little bit differently than his muckers and grinders, and when the guys who don't get all the notoriety see that, you don't get the most out of them. I'm a firm believer that the playoffs aren't a sprint; they are long—really long. For a winning team, they last two and a half months, and you need everybody. You can't go into a playoff series relying on two or three lines; you need all four. You need all your D. Everybody's got to play; otherwise, sooner or later, you'll just run out of gas, and when you get tired, you make mistakes. You have to keep your guys fresh.

The first thing I did after taking the job was to call a team meeting. A lot of teams will respond to a different voice in the short term, and I had to establish that we had strong leadership, contrary to talk around the league. "I hear that bullshit all the time," I said, "and I want you to know that you have a great captain right here in Scotty Stevens. Just because Scotty doesn't stand up and scream and yell doesn't mean that he's not a leader. He doesn't show his leadership that way. Who's the hardest worker on the ice? Who practises hardest? Who comes to play every night? Who hits? Who fights? Who does everything? You've got the greatest captain right here. We don't need to change anything!"

Right away, I established that I had total trust in his leadership. Of all the things that I did as a head coach, this was probably one of the best, because Scotty has a tremendous, tremendous amount of pride. Right away, by telling the group I was more than confident in Scott as our captain, that really helped.

After that speech, Scotty's game really changed, and we saw the type of player that he could be. Here was a guy who absolutely dominated the blue line throughout his career. There's a reason why he's in the Hockey Hall of Fame right now. For a guy who played the way he did, hit the way he did, and was as durable as he was—this is a specimen.

My meetings were a little different from Robbie's. He liked to go into the room after a game and talk to the guys, no matter what. If I went into the room, it was because I had something to say, but if there was nothing to say, then I let them be. The guys played hard, so I'd let them enjoy the moment. That was something that I believed in as a coach.

I also got tremendous support from the assistant coaches, like Bobby Carpenter, who did a great job. I relied on Carpy to work with the penalty killers, and Slava Fetisov worked with the power play. But Slava used to drive me nuts because he was never prepared: we would have set times for meetings and he would come in 15 minutes beforehand and start going over his tapes. I don't know what he did, but somehow, he got his point across and we had a great power play. Special teams are really important, especially during the playoffs, and we were sharp in both those areas. Slava and Carpy gave me the freedom to focus on other things.

After settling in, we just got back to the basics. I used ideas that we'd had with Jacques Lemaire and mixed them in with a few of my own. I felt we had been successful before because we were a really good defensive team, so we re-established that—and the team took off. We finished the season pretty strong, just behind the Flyers in the Atlantic Division.

To me, defensive hockey is also offensive hockey, because if you don't have the puck and you don't play good defence, you'll never get the puck back. If you want to get back on offence, then you've got to play good defence—they go hand in hand. When we played well positionally, we got the puck back right away. We had the puck all the time.

People also forget how many goals we scored. We might have been the best defensive team in the league, but we were also among the league leaders in scoring. I think a lot of getting tagged "Devils defence" was just frustration on the part of other teams because they couldn't break through us and get good scoring chances themselves.

In 1995, we hadn't been the fastest team in the league, but we had four really balanced lines. In 2000, we had three or four outstanding rookies: Brian Rafalski played with Scott Stevens and turned out to be one of the best blueliners on that team for many years. John Madden and Scotty Gomez were also rookies who added a lot to the team. We had the "A" line of Jason Arnott, Patrik Eliáš, and Petr Sýkora, and a dominant checking line: Bobby Holík, John Madden, and Randy McKay were simply incredible. I am still in awe of the job they did against the Leafs in the final game of the Eastern semifinal. As the coach, you get caught up in the game, changing lines, trying to get matches, and everything else. In the middle of the third, I took a quick look up at the clock, and I thought it said Toronto had 16 shots on us. I thought that was pretty good, but then I looked again and saw that it was only *six* shots. We were in the middle of the third period and Toronto only had six shots on goal! It was the most dominating checking experience I've ever seen in my life. Holík absolutely drove poor Mats Sundin crazy. And behind them, we had Scotty Stevens and Scotty Niedermayer. I can't say enough about those two.

Marty Brodeur was exceptional in goal, as always. Marty is a terrific athlete. No matter what he plays—golf, baseball, tennis—he excels. As a goaltender, he is a complete package: he passes the puck better than 80 per cent of the forwards in our league, and he is quick. Marty owes a lot of his career to Jacques Caron, because while Marty was already a great athlete and a good goaltender, Jacques made him a *great* goaltender. Jacques made him more of a standup goalie. Marty went down a little bit more early in his career, and Jacques told him that if he kept doing that, he wasn't going to have any knees left. That extended Marty's career. Jacques just had a way with Marty, knew how to talk to him, knew how to motivate him. Jacques was probably one of the most positive people that I've ever been around in my life, and he did wonders with Marty.

A lot of the guys, Scotty Stevens included, looked to Marty because it didn't take a rocket scientist to realize we weren't going anywhere unless we had Marty at the top of his game. The guy stood on his head. He worked every bit as hard in practice, too. He was like an old-school type of player in that he had fun in practices and would challenge the guys in a way that made them better. I played with Patrick Roy, and Patrick is one of the greatest to ever play the position, but if I were to name the best goaltender I've ever seen, I'd have to say it was Marty—Ken Dryden included.

We started the playoffs and got on a roll right away, beating the Panthers in four straight and then the Leafs in six. But then we were down three games to one against Philadelphia, playing in New Jersey. I knew we were a much better team than we were showing. I knew you couldn't let opportunities go by without taking advantage of them, thinking that you'll get another chance. I went into the room, and at first, I wasn't all that angry—I was more disappointed. Then, after getting everybody's attention, I started my little speech, and as I got going, I got more pumped up and more angry. I know there were an awful lot of expletives in that rant, but I got my point across.

When I look back on most series, there is always a turning point, and I think my rant was the turning point for us. It seemed that we all really came together at that moment. The guys proved to themselves that if they played the way they were capable of and stuck to the game plan, they could win it all. They won the next game and won the series.

Sometimes I would also use clips from movies to make my point. *Any Given Sunday* was one; *Remember the Titans* was another. Truthfully, the idea came from Lou, who happened to say, "I was watching a great movie. You've got to see it. It was very motivating." I don't think you can do that all the time, but as the playoffs moved ahead, the guys looked forward to them.

For me, it was an accomplishment to have everybody ready and everybody playing. I don't think fans really understand just how hard it is for coaches during a playoff series. When one game is over, no matter the outcome, you're immediately getting ready for the next one. For example, in the Philly series, it was 1:30 or two o'clock in the morning when, after repeatedly watching the game over and over, back and forth, I realized that the Flyers were doing the same thing on their forecheck. We made a bit of an adjustment in our play, which they didn't pick up, and that was one of the reasons we were able to come back. I was very proud that we adjusted and they didn't, and it made a difference.

If I got three or four hours of sleep a night, I was lucky. We didn't have the technology we have today, so I would work late into the night, preparing game films for the guys. It takes its toll; I see pictures of myself when I first started as a coach and then look at pictures of me during this series and I notice that the hair is a lot greyer. Anybody who says there's no stress involved in coaching isn't doing it.

We really had momentum by the time we played Dallas in the final. Claude Lemieux was feisty as hell, Scotty Stevens was banging bodies around, and Martin Brodeur was a wall in goal. It was a tough series, back and forth, and could have gone either way. Both Marty and Eddie Belfour, the Stars' goalie, were outstanding. The two teams were pretty evenly matched all over the ice.

We won Game One, 7–3, but the rest of the games were really close. The Stars won Game Two in New Jersey by a 2–1 score, but we took both games in Dallas. Game Five, in New Jersey, went into triple overtime with neither team having scored, and then Modano scored for the Dallas win. It was a shame that either team had to lose, it was such a close, dramatic game.

Game Six was played in Dallas, with us up three games to two in the series. Again we went into overtime, with the score tied at one. Then we went into a second overtime, in which Eliáš and Arnott hooked up on the winning goal. The next thing I know, Slava and I are jumping up and down, hugging each other. I went running across the ice, and don't know how the hell I didn't slip, but the celebration was unbelievable. Petr Sýkora had been hit with a dirty elbow by Derian Hatcher and had been taken to the hospital, so I grabbed Petr's sweater when we were taking pictures on the ice and threw it on over my jacket so that he would be part of the picture.

After the original emotion, I just needed a little time alone. All the guys were in the dressing room, celebrating with champagne, while I snuck out the back door. And who was standing there, outside the arena? Lou!

Lou and I decided we would take off and go to the hospital to see how Petr was doing while everybody was celebrating, and fortunately it turned out that he was fine. Then we went back and met everybody at the hotel and had something to eat. We spent the night in Dallas and left to go back to Jersey the next day, where the town had a big parade for us.

I will never forget that day—ever. Not only was it my first Stanley Cup as a head coach, but even more important, it was the day my first grandson, Dylan, was born.

When I reflect back, this was likely my greatest day in hockey. There was a whole different feeling winning the Stanley Cup as a head coach, as opposed to an assistant coach, and certainly different than winning it all as a player. As an assistant coach, you have responsibilities, but nowhere near those of a head coach. As head coach, you're not just feeling great for yourself, you're feeling great for 25 players who have just accomplished something that, in my case, I knew how they felt because I'd done it myself before.

When I got my day to spend with the Stanley Cup, I took it to my summer home in Plant City, Florida. There's a nice little restaurant there called Beef 'O' Brady's, and I knew the owner. When I asked him if I could bring the Cup there, he was ecstatic. People were lined up around the block to get a picture with me and the Stanley Cup. Funny enough, 80 per cent of the people who came out were from Michigan and were Detroit Red Wings fans.

I took the Cup over to our farm in Florida and got some pictures taken with the horses. Then we put Dylan, who was brand new and maybe six or seven pounds, right into the bowl of the Stanley Cup. He fit just perfectly, and those pictures are treasured.

CHAPTER 24

Breakdown

"Larry Robinson was a phenomenal person and player and coach. He's not too bad to have as a mentor. Between Scott Stevens and Larry Robinson, it's hard not to pick up a couple of useful tips or techniques from guys who only ever succeeded." – MARK FRASER, Edmonton Oilers

As the defending Stanley Cup champions, we were the team to beat in 2000–01. It was my team from the beginning, and we built on the momentum that we had generated the year before. We made very few roster changes. Really, the only significant difference was adding John Vanbiesbrouck to reinforce us in goal, although Marty still played almost all the games.

We still got tagged as a defensive club, but while defence was an important part of our game, we were the best offensive team in the NHL that season, and Patrik Eliáš and Alex Mogilny were both 40-goal scorers. All the guys played for me, and we finished the regular season on top of our division with 111 points.

But, as always, we had to work exceptionally hard through the playoffs. We got past the Carolina Hurricanes in six games, including two shutouts for Marty. He got another one in our seven-game series with the Toronto Maple Leafs, two of which went to OT. We beat the Pittsburgh Penguins in the conference final, which took five games, with Marty picking up two more shutouts. But in the end, we got our shot at the Stanley Cup again—this time against the Colorado Avalanche and my old teammate, Patrick Roy.

The series didn't start well. We stunk in the opener, a 5–0 loss, and early in the game, Randy McKay broke his hand in a hit with Ray Bourque. Fortunately, we were much better in Game Two, a 2–1 win.

We came home to New Jersey for Game Three, but we simply didn't work hard enough and didn't stick to our game plan. We ended up losing 3–1, and the fans got on us. We didn't have enough guys competing, and you are not going to win a lot of games when you only have eight or nine guys playing.

We were much better in Game Four. We kept going at Colorado, and it eventually worked in our favour when Roy misplayed a puck and Scott Gomez was able to score. We won 3–2. But on the first shift of the game, Jason Arnott had taken a puck to the face, and we ended up switching our lineup around for Game Five. I put Sergei Nemchinov between Sýkora and Eliáš and used Jim McKenzie in Arnie's place between Mogilny and Gomer. I also replaced Sean O'Donnell with Ken Sutton. It worked, and we won the game 4–1.

We left Denver needing just one win to repeat as Stanley Cup champions, and rather than have the guys check into a hotel back in New Jersey, I let them go home. It was the wrong move. Staying in a hotel away from the distractions of home would have kept everybody focused, but instead, the guys had the limos all ready, and they went out and celebrated. We lost our focus right there, and we got shut out. Hindsight is always 20/20, but that is one thing I'd like to have back.

Instead, it became winner-take-all in Denver for Game Seven, and the Avalanche took it all. Alex Tanguay beat us with a couple of goals and an assist, but we really beat ourselves. We competed better than we had in Game Six, but the thing that inevitably did us in was the same thing that we were guilty of the whole series, and that was taking stupid penalties. We were playing against a great team, and yet we were punching guys in the face for no reason. But we didn't have to be in Game Seven in the first place: I look at it more as though we lost the Cup in Game Six when we could have won it at home.

While we worked our tails off, it wasn't in the cards in 2001, and the Avalanche were determined to win the Stanley Cup for Ray Bourque, who had played his entire Hall of Fame career without winning it. Marty was tremendous in our goal, but Patrick Roy was sensational, and he won the Conn Smythe as the playoff MVP.

•

We had pretty much the same team in 2001–02, and I thought we should have been able to play with more consistency. I was trying to find different ways to motivate the guys and get them going, but the team just wasn't responding. I tried everything—we practised harder, we had no-puck practices—but no matter what, we were floundering. For over half a season, I was patiently hoping the guys would turn things around on their own, but Lou's patience ran out faster, and 51 games into the season, I was fired. Lou knew he had to make a change, and he hired Kevin Constantine to take my place.

When I was hired to replace Robbie Ftorck, I had been considered a players' coach replacing a strict disciplinarian. But now that I couldn't motivate the guys, Lou replaced me with a disciplinarian. It was hard for Lou to let me go, I know—as we had (and have) a great relationship—but Lou has to do what is right for the team, and that's what he felt he had to do.

John Cunniff, who had been coaching the Albany River Rats, was hired as an assistant to Kevin Constantine, but after John was diagnosed with cancer and got so sick that he couldn't keep going at the end of February, Lou called me. I was sitting in my car at the farm, and he asked me if I would come back to the team as an assistant coach because of the situation. I really didn't know what to do, so I called a friend of mine who works in human resources to ask her opinion. I knew what I wanted to do, and her advice was to follow my heart. I guess I needed somebody to confirm my thoughts, so, just a month after being let go from the Devils, I agreed to return to the team.

Though I was excited to be back behind the bench, it was one of my most difficult times in coaching because a lot of Kevin's philosophies were completely different from my own. Now, all of a sudden, I was doing things that he wanted to do—not stuff that I believe should be done. I did think Kevin did a great job in getting his point across: he was a very good speaker and held great meetings. But in hockey, you have to make adjustments on the go, and sometimes I would ask Kevin about certain things behind the bench and he wasn't able to answer me. He could only see things after he saw them on a video. A lot of times, I'd have to catch myself because I'd say to a player, "Why were you doing that? You shouldn't go there." And he would say, "Well, that's what Kevin wants us to do." I'd have to hold back: "Oh, sorry. That's right."

We ran practices differently, as well. For example, Kevin loved for both defencemen and forwards to block shots, and a lot of times during his practices, he'd bring out tennis balls and have guys going down to block. I saw all these guys in the dressing room with ice packs all over them, and asked, "What the heck is going on?" For me,

Larry Robinson Collection

Wayne Gretzky (left) and I were named co-captains of Team Canada in the 1984 Canada Cup tournament. It was a divided team, but we pulled it together and defeated Sweden to win the championship.

Paul Bereswill/Hockey Hall of Fame

By 1986, most of the boys who were part of our Stanley Cup wins during the seventies were gone, and Bob Gainey and I were the old guard of the team. We surprised everyone and won the Cup that year. It was Bob's fifth and my sixth Stanley Cup championship.

Hockey Hall of Fame

Considering how long I played hockey and how many Cups I got to win as a defenceman with Montreal, it was my first Stanley Cup win as a head coach that is actually my greatest day in hockey.

Larry Robinson Collection

In 1985, during the Canadiens' 75th anniversary, the team asked the fans to select their All-Time Dream Team. I was thrilled and honoured to be selected to join (left to right) Jacques Plante, Doug Harvey, me, Rocket Richard, Dickie Moore, Jean Beliveau and coach Toe Blake.

Miles Nadal/Hockey Hall of Fame

I took incredible pride in playing for my country when invited, and took part in the Canada Cup in 1976, 1981 and 1984, the World Championship in 1981 as well as several other games against teams from the Soviet Union.

Frank Prazak/Hockey Hall of Fame

I considered myself a physical player and suffered my fair share of injuries, but I didn't start wearing a helmet until after I was hit over the head by Wilf Paiement of the Nordiques.

Larry Robinson Collection

I discovered that polo was another sport I loved almost as much as hockey. I had always loved horses, but when Steve Shutt and I were introduced to the game, it became a new passion. Here I am on my mount beside Jeannette.

Larry Robinson Collection

I was named to Team Canada's roster for the Canada Cup in 1987, but broke my leg playing polo and missed not only that tournament but the first two months of the 1987–88 hockey season.

Doug MacLellan/Hockey Hall of Fame

In 1988, after sixteen seasons with the Canadiens, I ended my playing career with three seasons with the Los Angeles Kings. I occasionally question whether I should have left Montreal, but I am proud to say that I never missed the playoffs during my 20-season NHL career.

Kevin Shea

I was surprised yet pleased to have a road named after me in my hometown of Marvelville.

Andy Marlin/NHL/via Getty Images

I never dreamed that after I retired as a player, I'd become a coach. We won the Stanley Cup in New Jersey in 1995, in 2000 and in 2003.

Doug MacLellan/Hockey Hall of Fame

I dreamed of playing in the National Hockey League, but no one ever imagines that they'll one day be inducted into the Hockey Hall of Fame, but in 1995, that is what happened to me.

Doug MacLellan/Hockey Hall of Fame

The Hockey Hall of Fame Induction was a whirlwind, and I was so pleased that my family could be there to share it with me. Back row, left to right: my brother Moe, sister Carol, son Jeff, sister Linda and my brother Brian. Front row, left to right: Dad, Mom, me, Jeannette and daughter Rachelle.

The Montreal Canadiens are a class organization, and on November 19, 2007, they retired my number 19 in a ceremony before a game against the Ottawa Senators. My family was all there, and the amazing Montreal fans gave me a prolonged ovation that brought me to tears.

Rachelle Brehm/Larry Robinson Collection

One of the reasons I took the move to Los Angeles was to be closer to my grandchildren. We had a great time meeting monsters at Universal Studios' House of Horrors. Left to right are my son-in-law Larry Brehm, the twins Blake and Brian in front of Frankenstein, and me.

Larry Robinson Collection

During my playing career, I was away so much that I barely got to see my kids, Jeffery and Rachelle, grow up. I vowed to spend as much time as I can with my grandkids. My daughter-in-law Carol, Jeffery, me and Jeannette celebrate my grandson, Dylan's, baseball championship.

Larry Robinson Collection

Jeannette and I try to spend as much time with our grandkids as we can. We took the twins (Blake on the left, Brian on the right) to the Natural History Museum of Los Angeles County.

Rachelle Brehm/Larry Robinson Collection

Following my playing career, I invested in a Play It Again Sports franchise in Torrance, California with my daughter and son-in-law, Larry Brehm (left).

The Canadian Press/Graham Hughes

Many consider Montreal's 'Big Three' among the best blueliners ever to lace up a pair of skates. Left to right, Serge Savard, Guy Lapointe and me in June 2014 when the Canadiens announced that Guy's number 5 would be retired.

you didn't want guys like Joe Nieuwendyk blocking shots. During a game, you do what you have to do, but that's not the first thing I want him thinking about. A lot of the time, especially around the net, we were caught flailing around like fish out of water.

Another thing I found difficult was Kevin's dissection of a game. I would sit with him for two and a half hours watching film, and it was frigging ridiculous. Finally, I asked, "Do you mind if I just take my own film back?" I would go home, break down the tape, and write down five or six things that Kevin and the others hadn't even picked up. I knew right then and there that we looked at the game a lot differently. But I did my thing and they did theirs, and that's how the year went. Unfortunately, it led to us finishing sixth in the Eastern Conference and getting knocked out of the playoffs in the first round.

Unsurprisingly, Lou cleaned house and brought in Pat Burns for 2002–03. I chose to be a consultant, working with their minor-league system. I knew Pat well from playing for him in Montreal, and had a ton of respect for him, but I knew that he felt uneasy with me being around.

Burnsie was a tough, hard-ass guy. He knew the game fairly well, but he wasn't an Xs-and-Os guy, and he relied on Bobby Carpenter and, later, Jacques Laperrière to do all that kind of stuff. Burns was the line changer and the disciplinarian. He carried a big stick and he scared the crap out of a lot of guys, like Eliáš and Gomez, who were always on his list because they didn't play his type of game. They were more visual kind of guys, so that's where I'd take them aside, sit down with tapes, and go over stuff that would help them out.

Pat's time in New Jersey didn't last long, for unfortunate reasons. He was going through intensive treatments for colon cancer in 2003 and through what would have been the 2004–05 season—which was wiped out by the NHL lockout. He was doing much better, but then in July 2005, he was diagnosed with cancer for a second time. This time, it was in his liver. Pat was devastated. "I was feeling great, I was in top shape with great expectations," he said, shaking his head. "Then it showed up again in a CAT scan."

At a media conference, Lou announced, "Pat Burns will not coach next year." I was asked to return to coach the Devils, said yes, and was behind the bench once again to start the 2005–06 season. Meanwhile, Pat was going through his treatments in Punta Gorda, Florida, and was doing a little bit of scouting for the Devils. He came to Tampa to see us play the Lightning in late November that year. The guys were charged up to see him, and he was equally happy to see them.

But at the same time, I was getting to the point where the stress was catching up to me. I was plagued by headaches. I wasn't healthy, and it was the first time that I've ever been so sick that I couldn't go to a game. As a matter of fact, the doctor ended up coming to our apartment to give me some medication because I was so sick in bed. It was either walk away and get better, or risk getting to the point where I was going to be so sick that I couldn't function. That's when I decided to step down. I decided my health was more important than coaching the New Jersey Devils.

I broke down in Lou's office when I explained to him that I just couldn't keep on going. A lot of things were getting to me. I wanted the team to be successful, of course, but if I couldn't be at my best and it was bothering me healthwise, I couldn't do that. It was more than that, too: my daughter was pregnant with twins at the time, and I was worried about never seeing my family. As a coach, you're never home—you're always on the road and you're always at the rink. That's why I decided to step away.

On December 18, 2005, I resigned. The Devils announced that no immediate replacement had been named. Lou, the Devils' president and general manager, ran the practice the next day and ultimately decided that he would coach for the rest of the season.

I moved back to our home in Florida, then went out to California to visit my daughter after the twins were born. I don't think I watched hockey for two weeks, but not much longer than that—even though I had pulled myself away, I was still interested. I loved the guys, and wanted to see how they would respond to Lou behind the bench. When hockey is in your blood, it's nice sometimes to think you can get away from it, but that's a lot easier said than done.

In the meantime, Pat Burns and I kept in touch. When the Devils would play in Tampa, I would take him to the game. He was such a fabulous guy, and when he battled cancer a third time, it was all too clear just how sick he was. During the last months of his life, Pat sold off all of his motorcycles, and I bought one of them. He died in November 2010 after the colon cancer spread to his lungs.

Claude Julien was hired to coach the Devils for 2006–07 (having formerly coached my old team in Montreal), but history repeated itself. Once again, Lou felt he needed a change, and with three games left in the season, he fired Claude and went back behind the bench himself.

I wasn't away from the game very long. Lou approached me about returning to the Devils to assist Brent Sutter, whom he hired as coach during the summer of 2007. Although my role was different, in many ways it was as if I hadn't left. A lot of the same people were around, both players and staff. I have to admit that I was a little embarrassed to return after having had to resign because I hadn't been able to handle the pressure, but I still had a lot of confidence in my ability and what I could bring to the team. But Lou has been amazingly loyal; he knew what I had done for him, and vice versa. It was an easy adjustment for me.

The Devils went through a string of head coaches in the next few years. I worked with Jacques Lemaire once again during the 2009–10 season, and then John MacLean took over for 2010–11, but only lasted until December. Lemaire was brought back to finish the season.

Peter DeBoer came in for 2011–12, and I spent a very enjoyable year along with Dave Barr and Adam Oates, the other assistant coaches. I really liked Peter a lot—he was a great communicator—and got along extremely well with Barrsie and Oatesie. Adam is an extremely intelligent person, and very technical. He did a great job with the power play and had a good rapport with the guys. We had a tremendous year.

We were in the very competitive Atlantic Division, finishing with 102 points, but still in fourth place behind the Rangers, Penguins, and Flyers. In the first round of the playoffs, we faced the Florida Panthers and beat them in seven games—although it took a double-overtime goal by one of our rookies for us to move on. Then we beat Philadelphia in five games, followed by the Rangers in six. Another overtime goal, from Adam Henrique, gave us the Eastern Conference championship.

We had played the Kings, our opponents in the final, twice during the regular season, and beaten them both times. Because our regular-season point total was better than L.A.'s, we had the home-ice advantage in the series. Nonetheless, the Kings beat us in the first two games in New Jersey, both in overtime, leaving us in a sizable hole. And then, in Los Angeles for Game Three, they shut us out 4–0. With our backs against the wall, we fought back and won Game Four, 3–1, with all of our goals in the third period. Back at home in New Jersey for Game Five, we won 2–1.

But then there was Game Six.

Steve Bernier got a five-minute major and a game misconduct in the first period for charging Rob Scuderi of the Kings into the end boards. During the major, the Kings scored three goals, and we were never able to climb back. We lost the game, 6–1.

I believe that it wasn't left to the players to decide who won the game. It came down to a call by an official, and that should never be the case. I understand that officiating is a very, very tough occupation, because no matter what call you make, it's not going to be good for the one of the teams. But the way we lost, and to see Bernier's face when the call was made against him—that was very, very disappointing for me. There's still a bad taste in my mouth. My most disappointing moment was losing that Stanley Cup final to L.A. I felt that we were as good a team as the Kings and deserved a lot better.

My contract wasn't renewed by the Devils in the summer of 2012, but there were no hard feelings. We had enjoyed a wonderful history together, including two Stanley Cup championships and another trip to the Stanley Cup final. Lou and I have been great friends, and still remain great friends. I have immense respect for Lou, and owe a lot of my career to Lou Lamoriello for what he's done for me.

I'm a very emotional person, and unfortunately, emotion can sometimes get you into trouble. Sometimes, as a coach, you have to make decisions that are going to hurt people. I clearly recall a conversation I had with Lou Lamoriello that has resonated with me through the years. He said, "Never, ever confuse the player with the person." There's a difference. There's the player who can do things for you on the ice. If he's not doing it, then you have to discipline him in some way. That has nothing to do with the person. A person is something else. Lou told me never to confuse the two, and I've kept that with me throughout my career.

CHAPTER 25

Shark Thanks

"I'm a firm believer in positive reinforcement versus the negative, and Larry's a positive guy every day. Whether you're 36 or one of our younger defencemen, that positive attitude, with his knowledge, is very helpful." – DAN BOYLE

After the 2011–12 season, Marc Bergevin was hired as the general manager of the Montreal Canadiens, and I let it be known that I would be very interested in returning to Montreal as part of their coaching staff. Having played there for so many years, and with coaching experience under my belt, I had hoped that I might be considered. As it turned out, they hired J.J. Daigneault for the available position.

It had been a tremendously long year. The days were long themselves, and I think that through the entire season, we maybe had six days off. I was tired, physically and mentally. And I felt that I hadn't been fair to Jeannette—I was never home. I had seriously considered retiring, and asked my financial guys, "If I decide to retire, what kind of salary am I looking at?" We were also looking at health insurance because, in the United States, God forbid that something should happen. If you get deathly sick, the cost of hospitalization and treatment can very quickly wipe out your nest egg.

Then, out of the blue, I got a call from Murray Wilson, who had been a teammate of mine in Montreal. After exchanging pleasantries, he said, "Larry, my brother's been trying to get a hold of you." I was told that Doug, the GM of the San Jose Sharks, wanted to get some information about someone. I had no idea that that someone was me!

I had known Doug since he was probably 12 years old. He was a few years younger than Murray, and like me, they're both from the Ottawa area. Later on, I played against Doug when he was with the Blackhawks. Terrific defenceman. He had a great slapshot from the point.

I called Doug, and before I knew it, he had asked, "Would you be interested in joining the San Jose Sharks?"

"Yes, but on one condition," I told him. "I want to bring my wife to San Jose and get a chance to look around first. If she feels comfortable with it, then I'm comfortable with the move."

I had played or coached for so many years in the east, which was great for me personally because Jeannette and I got the chance to see our son, Jeffery, and his wife and our grandson, Dylan, fairly often. But we didn't get to see our daughter, Rachelle, and her husband and their twins, Blake and Brian, nearly as often, because they lived on the west coast. I thought a move to San Jose would be a good opportunity to see the twins. When the Sharks went on the road and I was away, Jeannette could head down and stay with our daughter and visit the boys. In addition, I had partnered with my son-in-law, Larry Brehm, and opened Larry Robinson's Play It Again Sports in Torrance, California, so my move to the west coast would put me closer to that business venture, too.

To that end, the move to San Jose was probably more a family move than it was a career move. Being closer to Rachelle and her family was very important to me and Jeannette. I signed a two-year contract as an assistant coach with the Sharks in July 2012, and the move to the west coast has worked out beautifully. Jeannette is very comfortable in San Jose and we both really enjoy it there.

The thing I love most about the organization is that it's so family-oriented. I had no idea until I got there, but it's terrific. The kids are encouraged to come down to the rink, and if you have people in from out of town, they are always welcomed.

The Sharks' coach, Todd McLellan, previously had great success at the junior level, and then won the Calder Cup with the Houston Aeros, Minnesota's American Hockey League affiliate, in 2003. He was hired as an assistant coach by the Detroit Red Wings in 2005 and was really key to their power play. After the Wings won the Stanley Cup in 2008, Dougie gave Todd the chance to be a head coach, which wasn't going to happen in Detroit with Mike Babcock there. The Sharks finished first overall in Todd's first season as a head coach, and have finished first in their division in his first three seasons.

I am very happy in my role as an assistant coach, and was not hired as a replacement in waiting, should Todd falter. I wouldn't want to be a head coach in that situation. I've *been* a head coach, and there are enormous pressures without the sword of Damocles hanging over your head.

The day after I was hired, the Sharks hired Jim Johnson, an NHL veteran who had been an assistant coach in Washington. It is our responsibility to work on team defence, and Jimmy's very good at designing drills, while I'm more the guy who picks up on the little things—like helping a guy with his stick positioning or noticing that a guy isn't upright enough. I have really enjoyed teaching younger guys like Justin Braun and Matt Irwin. They have really developed quickly, and because of that, we were able to be creative and move Brent Burns from the blue line up to the wing.

I think the key to coaching is to avoid trying to change somebody. Instead, you want to help them improve the way they already do certain things to make them more effective. For me, that was the biggest transition from being Larry Robinson the player to Larry Robinson the coach. You can't say, "I would have done it this way." That's not the way it works—you're not the one doing it.

I love being an assistant coach the most, in fact. I'm in a position where I can contribute. I was too emotional to be a head coach. I cared too much and I couldn't turn it off. It took its toll on me and I ended up making myself sick. I'm not in this industry to kill myself, so I figured I'd better change if I wanted to stay in the game.

Naturally, your head coach makes the final decisions, so Todd has the final say, but everybody on the coaching staff works well together in San Jose, and nobody is afraid of saying something. There are no egos. Truthfully, we all think pretty much the same way, so it's been a great fit for me.

I don't know how long I'll continue coaching. It depends on how my old body stands up to the rigours of another full season. We don't get any younger, and I still want to enjoy some of the life that we sacrifice by doing what we do in working in hockey.

CHAPTER 26

Hockey On Horseback

"There is no greatness without a passion to be great, whether it's the aspiration of an athlete or an artist, a scientist, a parent, or a business person." – ANTHONY ROBBINS

Back when I was living on the West Island of Montreal in the early 1980s, I looked around and didn't like some of the things I was seeing. I saw kids getting into things that made me uncomfortable. There were gangs of kids hanging out at the arcades, getting up to no good. I grew up on a farm and I wanted my kids to have the same values I was raised with.

At the time, Steve Shutt and Guy Lapointe had been talking about moving farther west of Montreal. In fact, Shutty bought a farm west of the city, moved there, and then bought a horse. I started thinking I'd like to do something similar, as I had spent my childhood around horses, so I started looking at places out that way, too. We ended up moving to Saint-Lazare, about 45 minutes southwest of downtown Montreal. Saint-Lazare has a sizable horse population, with a lot of residential properties dedicated to horse training and breeding.

The place that Jeannette and I bought hadn't been finished yet. I suddenly had a lot going on—I was building a barn and finishing a house. And then I ended up buying a horse, so I needed a place to board it. I found the Allards, a family that had a boarding stable about five minutes away.

My horse was trained western and I had a western saddle, so every time I'd go over to the Allards' stable, they'd say, "Oh, you're the cowboy that comes in." They later introduced me to five or six couples who had started the Montreal Polo Club, and when they found out I rode, they asked if I'd be interested in playing polo, and said they had a horse I could use to see if I liked it. Steve Shutt tried it, too, and we both fell in love with the sport. I ended up trading my western saddle for a polo saddle. I actually feel more comfortable in a flat polo saddle now.

Though I grew up on a farm and rode horses all my life, all of a sudden I found myself in a sport where I realized I had to teach the horse to be my feet. Polo is a stick-and-ball game, not unlike hockey in some ways, and is in fact often called "hockey on horseback." So Shutty and I had an advantage, as we had good hand-eye coordination and quick reflexes from playing hockey at an advanced level. We could anticipate the plays, but now, we had a 1,200-pound animal under us and we had to get it to go where we wanted to go.

Polo is a very social game, and it wasn't long before Jeannette and I got caught up in the polo world. We became very good friends with Julien and Celia Allard, and once I bought my first horse (of several), their daughter Linda would come over and look after the horses when I was on the road. Linda's our groom.

I took three years of clinics to learn how to ride, and the rest was simply time in the saddle. Every chance I got, I played, and we ended up having a pretty good club. A couple of pros were hired from the United States, and they played with us for a couple of years. Actually, one of the pros, Eddy Martínez, is still one of my best friends. Eddy comes from the Dominican Republic, and I thought I'd have some fun and got him on a pair of skates one time in Dorval. That was really fun to watch! He doesn't laugh at my polo skills anymore!

The object of polo is to score goals on the opposing team by using a long-handled mallet to hit the polo ball between two goal posts eight yards apart at each end of the field. The game, which is divided into four periods called chukkers, is played on a very large field 300 yards long and 160 yards wide. Each polo team consists of four riders, and each rider has a number with specific responsibilities. Number 1 is the most offence-oriented position on the field, but also covers the other team's Number 4. Number 2 can pass to the Number 1 and then get in behind him when heading towards a goal, or try to score themselves. The Number 2 also covers the opposing team's Number 3, who is usually the best player on the field. Number 3 controls the game and feeds balls to the Number 1 or 2, but must also be strong defensively. And the Number 4 is the primary player on defence. These players move anywhere on the field—but their principal responsibility is to stop the other team from scoring.

When you're first starting, you either play Number 1 or Number 4. Steve Shutt very naturally took to being a Number 1, where you're up front and you score all the goals. I've played Number 4 pretty well my entire polo career. I'm responsible for covering the other team's Number 1, keeping the back door closed and getting the ball out to our Number 3.

Each player wears a helmet, a coloured shirt with the number of the player's position, white pants, and riding boots. The mallet has a cigar-shaped head about nine inches long, with a grip and a sling that you wrap around your thumb. The polo ball is struck with the broad sides of the mallet head, not the round and flat tips.

Even though they're called polo ponies, they are actually full-sized horses, and they're chosen for their speed, agility, and stamina. They're trained to be handled with one hand on the reins, and you use your legs to direct them. Each player plays the entire game—there are no substitutions—but we use several horses through each match. Most of the time, we change mounts between chukkers. This is why we require more than one horse, and as many as six altogether.

Polo is reputed to be the second-most dangerous sport to race-car driving. It's not for the faint of heart, that's for sure, and it is rare to find a hockey player who plays polo. I still play when I can, but Shutty hasn't played in probably 15 years now. It's a really expensive sport, too. I had six mounts at one time, and each of them cost in the neighbourhood of $5,000 up to $50,000. And horses are expensive to board, feed and train. Back when I started, a bag of food cost four dollars; it's 12 now. A bale of hay was two dollars, and now it's 10 or 11 bucks. And when I first started, you could shoe a horse for probably $60 or $70. Now, it's $110 just to shoe one horse.

Polo is truly a serious endeavour for me—not just a hobby. I still play when I get a chance, but the hockey schedule overlaps with polo season. The last tournament in Sarasota, Florida (where I'm a member), begins the second week of April, and then the competition moves up to Ocala and finishes in mid-May. Because the hockey team has moved forward in the playoffs, I've missed everything.

I've had a few accidents playing polo. You're travelling at a speed of 25 or 30 miles per hour, and if something happens, there are six or seven horses coming behind you at the same speed. If you fall, it usually results in a separated shoulder . . . at the very least.

Once, in a match my team played against a team from New York, I was going to goal, and there was a guy in goal coming towards me. The rules in polo dictate that everything to the left of the ball within 10 feet is the right of way. I got bumped and my horse crashed into the side of the guy coming towards me, with my leg stuck in between. My teammates asked whether I was all right, and I admitted that it hurt a bit. I must have a high pain threshold, because I wrapped it with an Ace bandage, got back on my horse, and played two more chukkers.

When the match ended and I got off my horse, my leg was pounding, so I took the Ace bandage off and looked at it—and told my wife that she'd better get the car, because we were heading to the hospital. What happened was that, on the initial contact, I must have cracked my tibia, and by continuing to ride I displaced the fracture. When they X-rayed the leg, they clearly saw that the bone was displaced, so they had to put in two screws and do a bone graft.

Before the surgery, the doctor told me not to worry, that he'd talk to Serge about my leg and the operation. Later, when I was in recovery, filled with anaesthetic and painkillers, a photographer from one of the papers must have snuck in and taken some photos. The next day, the newspaper ran a big spread with a photo of a woozy me and a headline that asked, ROBINSON—SOON RETIRED?

I used that newspaper article as motivation, and was determined to get myself back on the ice as quickly as was safely possible.

Right after the operation, I was in a passive movement machine. By the third or fourth day, I was at 80 per cent flexion in my leg, and I was riding a bike 17 days later.

I owe it all to Gaétan Lefebvre, our trainer with the Canadiens. Gaet arranged to get a van from one of the local dealerships and took out the seats because I couldn't bend my leg with the brace they had on it. He'd pick me up at ten to seven in the morning and drop me off at seven o'clock at night. In between, we went to the Forum to work out, biking and building up my leg. Then we'd sneak across the street to the Alexis Nihon Plaza, where they had a pool. I wasn't allowed to put all of my weight on the leg, so we did a lot of exercises in the water. I was so grateful to Gaétan for working so diligently with me.

It was an unfortunate accident, however, and even more unfortunate timing, as it happened just before the start of the 1987–88 season. And while I was rehabilitating the leg, I suffered shin splints and had to undergo more tests. Serge told me to take all the time I needed to recover and be at 100 per cent, but as it was, I missed 27 games from the start of that season, which really put me behind.

Despite it all, polo remains a passion for me. It's a fascinating, frustrating game. While you know what you want to do, you can't always get the horse to go where you need to be.

CHAPTER 27

Reflections

"When you're not only respected but liked, that is a very unique situation, and he has both."

— LOU LAMORIELLO

I've lived a charmed life; of that, there is no doubt.

No one, and I mean *no one,* saw that skinny kid driving the tractor on the farm in Marvelville and predicted, "That boy is destined for greatness."

By the time I was a teenager, I was tall and awkward, both socially and athletically, but what I did have was a strong work ethic. Working on a farm for your family will do that to you. I worked long, hard days to accomplish the things that had to be done. And that formula worked for me as both a player and a coach. I was never afraid of hard work in any aspect of my life.

Throughout my NHL career, I never thought about personal awards. The only award that I ever really thought about was the Stanley Cup. It's not a personal award; it's a team award. That's the way I was raised: the team always comes first, and you're only ever as good as the guy sitting next to you.

Don't get me wrong—it's not that I'm not immensely proud of any award I've received. Winning the Norris Trophy and being named the best defenceman in the league is quite an honour. Being named to All-Star teams is a tremendous honour. But for me, a team victory is much more satisfying. At the end of the season, if our team hadn't won the Stanley Cup, we weren't successful. It was as simple as that. If we didn't win the Cup, the individual awards were more or less meaningless.

You have to have a lot of help to win honours like the Norris and the Conn Smythe, and not from just your teammates but at home, as well. The support I received was phenomenal. In fact, I think winning those awards was possibly more of an honour for my family and kids. I am very proud of having been selected to win the awards, but it's not something that I dwell on. In fact, the only really good thing that they did for me was to get me better contracts.

I am extremely proud of the records that I have, but records are established so that people will break them. When that happens, I'll gladly tip my hat to the guy who can accomplish it. Will someone ever break Gretzky's record for goals in a season? Hard to imagine that anybody can beat 92 goals. But no one thought that anybody would ever collect more career shutouts than Terry Sawchuk's 103, and yet Marty Brodeur came along and did just that. And he's still going. You can never say never. Having said that, it will take a huge accomplishment to equal my career plus/minus mark of plus-730. I was never a minus-player during my 20 seasons in the NHL. In 1976–77 alone, I was plus-120.

In this era, a really good season—I mean, a *really* good season—sees a guy with a plus-30. A player would have to have 25 seasons like that to beat the record. That is unlikely to happen. I'm not saying it won't ever be equalled, but it would be an extraordinary feat. That's the one record that I feel most confident of keeping.

I hold another record that I'm proud of, and that is reaching the playoffs in 20 straight seasons. I played a total of 20 seasons in the NHL and never once missed the playoffs. Nicklas Lidström has already tied the record, but now that he has retired, he won't be able to break it. Mark Messier only got to 18.

Both of those records have my name on them, but in truth, they're team records. No one can accomplish records like these without great teams around them.

I've been awarded and rewarded through the years, but when you are identified by Wayne Gretzky as a member of his all-time All-Star team, you are proud yet humbled. This is, after all, arguably the greatest player in the history of the game. In his autobiography, he wrote: "Here is my All-Star Team of players I've played with and against. This is based not only on talent but what they've done for the game, how much class they've shown and how tough they were in the clutch. Goalie: Grant Fuhr. Defence: Larry Robinson (classiest man alive), Paul Coffey. Forward: Mark Messier, Mario Lemieux, Gordie Howe.

How great is that?

During the team's 75th anniversary, the Montreal Canadiens honoured their All-Time Dream Team. Twenty thousand fans participated in a vote, naming the players they considered the best of the best through the history of the team. The fans selected Jacques Plante in goal, Jean Béliveau at centre, Maurice Richard at right wing, Dickie Moore at left wing, and I was incredibly honoured to be chosen, with Doug Harvey, as the top defencemen in the eyes of the fans. Toe Blake was chosen as the best coach.

There was an extraordinary number of Stanley Cup championships represented there on the ice. As players, Plante had won six,

Jean had 10, the Rocket had eight, Dickie had six, Doug had six, and, to that point, I had won five Cups.

They held a special ceremony on January 12, 1985. I was still playing at the time; the only active player selected to this elite team. Public address announcer Claude Mouton introduced each of us and recounted some of our accomplishments, and then, wearing our home jerseys, we made our way to centre ice. I have to tell you that it was incredibly humbling to stand beside these legends who had created indelible memories for the fans, established records, and, eventually, had been inducted into the Hockey Hall of Fame. As part of the ceremony, each of us, one by one, skated in on Plante and took a half-hearted shot, much to the delight of the fans. I lofted an easy wrist shot that Jacques caught.

Once we were introduced, they brought out Aurèle Joliat. Aurèle was the oldest alumnus of the Montreal Canadiens. He joined the team in the 1922–23 season, yet there he was, 83 years old and nimbly skating out, wearing a black cap like the one he had worn during his playing career. Aurèle stumbled over a mat that had been placed on the ice surface, but got right up, skated in on Plante for all he was worth, just like he might have in the 1920s, and Plante let him score. Aurèle was ecstatic! He celebrated like he had just scored the Stanley Cup–winning goal in overtime and did a lap of the ice. It was great to see.

The next night, the Canadiens held a fundraising dinner to raise money for children who are physically challenged. Such a great cause.

That whole week was a whirlwind. To be honest, I didn't appreciate the honour as much then as I do now. I look at all the great players who went through the Canadiens system, and all of a sudden I'm considered one of the best to have played for the team? It's pretty amazing when you really think of it. When I look back on it now, I was there with Aurèle Joliat and Dickie Moore and Maurice Richard and Jean Béliveau and Doug Harvey and Jacques Plante. Those are frigging icons! I was thinking, "What's this little farm boy doing up with all these guys?" It was amazing!

It's something that I'll cherish forever, but really, there are always going to be comparisons. For example, *The Hockey News* came out with the top 100 players ever to play the game. You look at all the different people who contribute to the selections, and of course, everybody has different opinions. It's extremely hard. How can you compare Jacques Plante to Martin Brodeur? They played in different eras. Is one any better than the other? Jacques Plante, when he played, was one of the greatest goalies ever to play. I think that Martin Brodeur is one of the best that I've ever seen since I've been involved in hockey. How can you compare?

And who's to say that I'm any better than Serge Savard? Who's to say that I'm any better than Guy Lapointe? It's just somebody's opinion. You can't compare. Don't get me wrong, I'm extremely, extremely honoured. I find it very humbling only because hockey is a team game. It's not tennis. It's not a sport like golf, where it's you against the course. I had to rely on Serge, and Serge had to rely on me. We both had to rely on Lafleur, and Lafleur had to rely on us. We both had to rely on Kenny Dryden, and Kenny on us. We all had to rely on each other. Who's to say one is any better than the other? Would I have been the same player if I hadn't played with Serge Savard? Who knows? But it certainly is a great honour, something I'll cherish forever.

There are a couple of other honours that I've received closer to home. There's the Metcalfe Arena, which has been renamed in my honour, and then there is Larry Robinson Road in Marvelville. I guess they ran out of names! Truth be told, I didn't even know they were doing that. I don't know if it had anything to do with my dad or my brother or whatever, but all I know is that somebody made a motion to name the road after me. My wife and I were driving home one summer, and we just happened to come to the corner and look up. There was Larry Robinson Road. That's how I first found out about it. I actually lived on the street. Our farm was a hundred feet up from the intersection where the two Larry Robinson Roads intersect. There's a bridge right there. To be honest with you, there aren't a lot of roads around there. Still, it is quite an honour.

On November 20, 1995, I was inducted into the Hockey Hall of Fame. Also inducted that year were Bun Cook in the Veteran category and Bill Torrey and Günther Sabetzki in the Builder category.

I remember getting the call informing me that I was being inducted. I was thrilled beyond belief, but I think my family was even more excited than I was. Then I remember talking to Red Fisher, the hockey writer for the Montreal *Gazette*. He told me, "Larry, you made the Hall of Fame, but I didn't vote for you."

I laughed and said, "That's okay, Red, I didn't need your vote."

Red started to laugh, and that's been our ongoing joke through the years. Red is a guy I absolutely respect. I love him dearly. He is a good man; a really good man.

One of the absolutely greatest honours of my hockey life was having my number retired by the Montreal Canadiens. It was a hugely emotional evening, and one that I am incredibly proud of and humbled by, and so happy I could share it with my family, some dear friends, some former teammates, and with the city of Montreal.

I retired from playing at the end of the 1991–92 season with the L.A. Kings. I had left the Canadiens after the 1988–89 season. No one wore the number 19 after I left Montreal, although I understand Jassen Cullimore asked to wear the number when he arrived in Montreal in 1996–97, but was denied. Yet the number wasn't retired until November 19, 2007, in a ceremony before a game against the Ottawa Senators at the Bell Centre.

When you first lace up your skates as a child, you dream of pulling on an NHL jersey. To wear a Canadiens jersey, with its fabled crest, made the dream that much more special for me. For generations, the names on the back of the jerseys that had been retired were the same ones that filled the league's record books. Never did I imagine that I might be one day honoured among them.

Just think about these names and their retired numbers:

Number 1: Jacques Plante
Number 2: Doug Harvey
Number 3: Émile "Butch" Bouchard
Number 4: Jean Béliveau
Number 5: Bernie Geoffrion
Number 7: Howie Morenz
Number 9: Maurice Richard
Number 10: Guy Lafleur
Number 12: Dickie Moore and Yvan Cournoyer
Number 16: Henri Richard and Elmer Lach
Number 18: Serge Savard
Number 29: Kenny Dryden

And then, after me, Bob Gainey's number 23 and Patrick Roy's number 33 were also retired and raised to the rafters in the Bell Centre.

To have your number retired by the Montreal Canadiens is one of the ultimate honours that a hockey player can achieve. You have to be considered one of the defining players in the franchise's history. Look at that list! Some of them were teammates of mine, but all of them are legends. I am humbled to know that my name will forever be included in such elite company. To be included in that same list is beyond a dream.

It was an incredibly emotional day for me. In fact, I still get emotional when I think about it. But it was also bittersweet for me. There were three things missing from the event: my mother, my father, and my brother. I would love to have had my parents there to enjoy the ceremony. They made so many sacrifices that helped my brothers, my sisters, and me to reach our dreams and succeed on the career paths that we chose. The Canadiens had talked about retiring my number for many years, but both Mom and Dad and my oldest brother, Brian, had passed away by the time the ceremony took place. Nevertheless, it is an honour that you can never take for granted.

The Canadiens appropriately chose the 19th of November to retire my jersey. The date, of course, corresponded with my jersey number, but playing against Ottawa, which is so close to my hometown, was also special. I was also very, very honoured that the Senators chose to be out on the ice during the ceremony. That was a very classy move on their part.

I was given plenty of notice, so I was able to invite everybody that I really felt strongly about to be there with me. When the Canadiens were thinking about having someone introduce me, I think everybody assumed it would be Serge Savard. I thought about several different people, but by that point, I had gone from being a player to a coach, and with it, my whole life had changed. I decided that I wanted Lou Lamoriello, whom I admire as much as anyone else in hockey, to speak on my behalf, and I was honoured when he agreed.

I was so pleased that my two sisters and my brother Moe were able to attend, and, of course, Jeannette with our children, Jeffery and Rachelle, and their spouses. And it was especially gratifying to have my three grandchildren—Dylan and the twins, Brian and Blake—right there beside me that day. They were pretty young at the time, but now they can visit the Bell Centre and see their grandfather's name and number high above the ice for years to come.

Dylan had just turned seven. He was born and raised in Florida, and it was the first time he had ever seen snow. My brother-in-law took him out to one of the parks and Dylan lay down in the snow and made snow angels.

There was a reception before the ceremony, and while I was nervous and anxious, it was incredibly reassuring to look around the room and see my family, some former teammates—including Guy Lafleur and Serge Savard—as well as the great Jean Béliveau there for an evening in my honour. The team presented me with a Michel Lapensée painting and a specially designed watch in an engraved case.

Just before the ceremony, they led my family to seats on a red carpet on the ice surface, but my oldest grandson, Dylan, stayed with me for a few minutes in the Canadiens' dressing room. We were both wearing Canadiens home jerseys with the alternate captain's A on the left breast and ROBINSON and my number 19 on the back. I could only shake my head and smile—Dylan was clutching a Big Bird doll that someone had given him.

I showed Dylan where all the boys used to sit—Flower, Shutty, Pointu, Sarge, Kenny—and where his grandpa sat and got dressed before every home game. I pointed out the photos and the John McCrae quote painted on the wall of the dressing room: *To you from failing hands we throw the torch. Be yours to hold it high.*

While Dylan and I were preoccupied in the dressing room, Dick Irvin and Richard Garneau, two marvellous broadcasters, were doing introductions on the ice. Then, when Dick introduced me, I took Dylan's hand and, followed by a camera crew, we made the short walk to the ice surface.

The crowd was on its feet, cheering, as I stepped onto the ice with Dylan. But I couldn't believe it—they didn't stop. I waved to every corner of the rink, but they continued to cheer. I'm a humble guy, and the cheering, which just got louder and continued, made me a little embarrassed and flustered. I tried to settle the fans down, but the cheering went on. And then, they started to chant, "Larry! Larry! Larry!" I was astonished and, candidly, taken aback. I loved the fans in Montreal and certainly knew that they appreciated me, but this was stunning. The fans refused to stop in spite of my trying to use hand gestures and then sitting down to get them to stop.

As if I wasn't emotional enough before, the ovation certainly reinforced that for me. It went on for a full five minutes.

The announcers outlined my career highlights in both French and English and acknowledged the incredible legacy of the Canadiens: the 24 Stanley Cups and the 12 players whose jerseys had already been retired.

While I glanced around at the thousands of faces in the arena, I noticed that all of the current Canadiens were wearing my number 19, too.

And then, Lou Lamoriello was introduced. The fans loved that Lou began by speaking a few words in French, and even through his accent, they were still recognizable.

Lou was very flattering when he said, "I always knew Larry Robinson the player, but it wasn't until 1993, when he joined the New Jersey Devils organization as an assistant coach under Jacques Lemaire, and later as a head coach himself, that I experienced his leadership, along with his teaching and coaching ability."

I was fortunate to win the Stanley Cup six times with the Montreal Canadiens as a player, and then, with Lou Lamoriello and the Devils, I won the Stanley Cup on three other occasions. Tears welled up in my eyes when Lou added that I was one of the most caring and considerate individuals with whom he had ever been associated.

Lou concluded his introduction by saying, "Tonight marks another moment in Larry's brilliant career. He was one of a kind on the ice, and he's one of a kind off the ice."

As I reflect on that evening today, it makes me realize just how fortunate I've been. So many people contributed to any success I might have enjoyed through my hockey career.

I had wonderful coaches who devoted their time to guys like me, and that goes all the way back to my days playing minor hockey in Russell, Ontario, right through junior, then on to Al MacNeil when I turned pro in Halifax, and all through my NHL career—Scotty Bowman, Boom Boom Geoffrion, Claude Ruel, Bob Berry, Jacques Lemaire, Jean Perron, Pat Burns, and Tom Webster. I learned something from every one of them.

Through my coaching career, I can't hold anyone in higher regard than Lou Lamoriello. He saw something in me and has been exceptionally loyal to me for many years, and I appreciate his support and friendship more than he'll ever know.

I learned how to win with the Montreal Canadiens. The idea of winning is ingrained into that *bleu, blanc, et rouge* jersey the second you pull it on. There is an extraordinary tradition that needs to be upheld by every player as they pass through the door of that dressing room. We stand on the shoulders of giants: the Rocket, Dickie Moore, Jacques Plante, Doug Harvey, Jean Béliveau, Henri Richard.

My teammates supported me as I did them, no matter which jersey I was wearing, but the success we enjoyed in Montreal makes that period of my life extra special. There is a bond of brothers there. Fred Shero was a man who I respected but desperately wanted to beat when he was coaching the Philadelphia Flyers, but there is a quote of his that resonates with me: "Win today and we walk together forever." While our post-hockey careers have taken us on varied paths, I'll forever be connected with the boys who joined me in celebrating those Stanley Cup victories: Flower and Coco, Shutty and Bo, Pointu and the Senator, Kenny and Bunny.

I consider Kenny Dryden's *The Game* to be the finest hockey book ever written. He captured what it was like to be a player, and a player with the Canadiens, in a manner that no one before or since has been able to do. His eloquence never surprised those of us who shared a dressing room with him.

In that book, Kenny described playing behind me, and I'm as flattered as any player can be:

> He was the rare player whose effect on a game was far greater than any statistical or concrete contribution he might make. When he came onto the ice, the attitude of the play seemed to change. Standing in back of him, I could feel it, I could see it change, growing more restrained, more respectful, as if it was waiting for him to see what he would do. Nowhere was this more clear, or more important, than against the Flyers or the Bruins. They held him in such awe, treating him with an embarrassing, almost fawning, respect, that they seemed even to abandon their style of play when he was around, and with it any hope of winning.

I loved everywhere I've lived, but I have a special affection for Montreal. The people of Montreal warmly welcomed an anglophone farm boy from Marvelville and made him fall in love with their city. It's an amazing city, and I was honoured to play there. In fact, if I have any regrets, it's that I didn't finish my career in Montreal.

My father and my older brother Brian were my heroes as a kid. Actually, I'll take that back. While both are no longer with us, they still serve as my heroes today.

There is one person, above and beyond all the others, who has allowed me to achieve the success that I did: Jeannette.

I was a skinny 18-year-old living on dreams when I met Jeannette. She is my best friend and the love of my life, and she put up with all the travelling, my bad moods, and everything else a professional athlete goes through to allow them to be the best that they can be. Unless they have a good, solid foundation at home, most people don't have the opportunity to reach the level of success I was able to achieve. Jeannette was the reason for my being up there.

Jeannette and I had to get married early, and young marriages often don't last. But we have survived all the trials and tribulations that we've been through. I wouldn't be anywhere near the person I am today if I hadn't been with Jeannette. She's been my rock. She's held our family together. It's never been about her. It's been whatever I wanted and she followed.

There's nobody more important than the person you live with twenty-four hours a day. With the careers that we have as professional athletes, your partner is not just a wife; she's also both father and mother to our kids, she's the friend, the business partner, the banker, the cook, the housekeeper, and everything else, because as players, we're going all the time. We simply don't have time to do much of anything but play hockey. When I got sent from the minors to play in Montreal, Jeannette had to pack up our life and move the family. When I was on the road, she was there at two in the morning when I got home, and then got up to drive the kids to school or take them to hockey practice when I couldn't be there. She's had to do it all.

I would have to say that the greatest awards I ever received were much more personal than the hockey honours I received. To have an amazing wife, who stood beside me through thick and thin, through my moods and our moves, was an exceptional gift. It's tough to be a hockey player's wife, but behind every successful hockey player, there's also a great woman. Jeannette has been my rock. She still is.

We've been blessed with two wonderful children, Jeffery and Rachelle. They may be the greatest gifts of all. They've been such an inspiration to me, and along with their spouses, Carol and Larry, they have blessed us with three wonderful grandchildren, whom we adore.

Time has flown far more quickly than I can even imagine, and the years have evaporated in a blur.. I was actually quite astonished when working on this book at just how many of my memories were intact after all these years. Certainly, I had to research many of the facts, but the stories rolled quite easily. I don't wish that I could relive any of them, but I wish I could have harnessed the years when my kids were young and enjoyed more time savouring the special moments in their childhood. I was there when I could be, but I've always held family up as the most important part of my life, and I now make certain that I spend as much time as I can with Dylan and the twins, and relish every opportunity.

I appreciate every opportunity I've been given, enjoyed every moment I've experienced and am thankful to everyone who has played a role in the life, on the ice and off, of Larry Robinson.

NHL TIMELINE

JUNE 2, 1951

Larry Clark Robinson is born in Winchester, Ontario.

JUNE 10, 1971

The Montreal Canadiens select Larry Robinson with the 20th overall selection in the NHL Amateur Draft.

JANUARY 8, 1973

Twenty-one-year-old defenceman Larry Robinson makes his NHL debut with Montreal in a 3–3 tie against the visiting Minnesota North Stars.

JANUARY 17, 1973

Larry Robinson scores his first career NHL point (an assist) in a 6–4 win against the Pittsburgh Penguins, in Montreal.

FEBRUARY 3, 1973

Larry Robinson scores his first NHL goal in a 7–1 Canadiens win over the Kings, at Los Angeles.

APRIL 17, 1973

In Game Two of the Stanley Cup semifinals, Larry Robinson scores the first playoff goal of his NHL career at 6:45 of overtime, giving the Canadiens a 4–3 win over the visiting Philadelphia Flyers. Robinson becomes just the second NHL rookie defenceman to score an overtime goal.

MAY 10, 1973

Rookie defenceman Larry Robinson wins his first Stanley Cup championship when Montreal beats the Black Hawks 6–4 in Chicago in Game Six of the final.

OCTOBER 9, 1974

Montreal defenceman Larry Robinson picks up a career-high 19 penalty minutes (17 of them in the third period, after a fight with Denis Potvin) in a 5–5 opening-night tie against the visiting New York Islanders.

JANUARY 23, 1975

Larry Robinson scores the milestone 10,000th goal in franchise history as the Canadiens beat the North Stars 7–0 at Minnesota.

FEBRUARY 12, 1975

Larry Robinson scores a goal and adds an assist as the Canadiens extend their NHL-record road undefeated streak to 17 straight games (10–0–7) with a 2–2 tie against the Maple Leafs, at Toronto.

NOVEMBER 15, 1975

Larry Robinson scores his 100th career NHL point with an assist to lead Montreal to a 4–4 tie against the visiting Chicago Black Hawks.

MAY 16, 1976

Larry Robinson wins his second Stanley Cup championship when Montreal beats Philadelphia 5–3 to sweep the best-of-seven final series in Game Four. It is the Canadiens' 19th title.

MARCH 3, 1977

Larry Robinson has two assists to tie and then set a new franchise record for most assists in a season by a defenceman in a 5–1 win over the visiting Penguins. His second assist breaks the mark of 52 set by J.C. Tremblay in 1970–71.

MARCH 14, 1977

Larry Robinson sets another franchise record for defencemen when his assist (in a 3–0 win over the visiting L.A. Kings) gives him 76 points on the season, breaking the mark set by Guy Lapointe in 1974–75.

APRIL 3, 1977

Larry Robinson picks up an assist in a 2–1 season-ending victory at Washington to finish the 1976–77 season with a plus/minus rating of plus-120, best in the NHL.

MAY 14, 1977

Larry Robinson has an assist on the first goal and wins his third Stanley Cup championship when the Canadiens defeat the host Boston Bruins 2–1 in Game Four of the final.

JUNE 6, 1977

Larry Robinson is named to the NHL First All-Star Team for the first time in his career.

JUNE 8, 1977

Larry Robinson wins the Norris Trophy, presented to the NHL's best defenceman, for the first time in his career.

MARCH 9, 1978

Larry Robinson leads the scoring with four assists in a 4–1 win over the visiting Toronto Maple Leafs.

MAY 16, 1978

Larry Robinson sets a team record for defencemen when his two assists give him 15 for the playoff year, breaking the mark of 14 set by J.C. Tremblay in 1971. The record comes in a 3–2 overtime win against the visiting Boston Bruins in Game Two of the final.

MAY 25, 1978

Larry Robinson picks up two assists and is named winner of the Conn Smythe Trophy (as playoff MVP) and wins his fourth Stanley Cup title when Montreal wins 4–1 at Boston in Game Six of the final.

JUNE 14, 1978

Larry Robinson is named to the NHL's Second All-Star Team.

OCTOBER 11, 1978

Larry Robinson scores a goal and two assists as the Habs beat the visiting Minnesota North Stars 5–2 to set an NHL record for longest opening-night undefeated streak (16 games; 12–0–4). They also become the first NHL team to win 1,100 home games.

JANUARY 29, 1979

Larry Robinson scores twice and adds two assists to lead Montreal to a 7–3 win at Philadelphia.

APRIL 22, 1979

Larry Robinson scores twice, including the winner on a power play at 4:14 of overtime, for a 5–4 win at Toronto in Game Four of the Stanley Cup quarterfinals.

MAY 5, 1979

Larry Robinson scores a goal and adds two assists to lead the Canadiens to a 5–1 win over the visiting Boston Bruins in Game Five of the Stanley Cup semifinals.

MAY 21, 1979

Larry Robinson wins his fifth Stanley Cup championship as Montreal beats the New York Rangers 4–1 in Game Five of the final.

JUNE 11, 1979

Larry Robinson is named to the NHL's First All-Star Team for the second time.

DECEMBER 15, 1979

Montreal's 22-year-old rookie defenceman, Moe Robinson, plays in the only game of his NHL career, replacing his injured older brother Larry as the Canadiens lose 6–2 in Winnipeg in their first-ever NHL road game against the Jets.

FEBRUARY 16, 1980

Larry Robinson has four assists as the Canadiens improve their undefeated home streak against Pittsburgh to 33 games (30–0–3) with an 8–1 win.

MARCH 22, 1980

Larry Robinson scores twice and adds two assists as the Canadiens tie the visiting Hartford Whalers 5–5.

JUNE 5, 1980

Larry Robinson wins the Norris Trophy for the second time in his career.

JUNE 9, 1980

Larry Robinson is named to the NHL's First All-Star team for the third time in four years.

NOVEMBER 11, 1980

Larry Robinson scores a goal and three assists to lead the Montreal Canadiens to an 8–2 win over the Colorado Rockies in Denver.

DECEMBER 27, 1980

Larry Robinson becomes the second defenceman in Montreal history to score 100 goals as the Canadiens extend their all-time home record against the Washington Capitals to 18–0–0 with a 7–4 win.

APRIL 9, 1981

Larry Robinson breaks Guy Lapointe's team record for defencemen with 69th playoff point of his career (an assist). He reaches the milestone in a 3–1 loss to the visiting Oilers in Game Two of their preliminary-round series.

JUNE 10, 1981

Larry Robinson is named to the NHL's Second All-Star Team for the second time in his career.

OCTOBER 27, 1981

Larry Robinson scores a goal and three assists as the Canadiens win 11–2 against the visiting Philadelphia Flyers.

DECEMBER 29, 1981

Larry Robinson picks up a goal and an assist in a 5–4 win over the Islanders in New York to give him 501 points in his NHL career.

MARCH 9, 1982

Larry Robinson picks up the 407th assist of his career, all with the Canadiens, in a 4–2 win over the visiting Boston Bruins. He breaks the team record of 406 established earlier in the season by Guy Lapointe.

FEBRUARY 27, 1983

Larry Robinson sets a franchise record for defencemen when his assist (in a 4–4 tie at Detroit) gives him 573 career points with the Canadiens, breaking the mark held by Guy Lapointe.

NOVEMBER 19, 1984

Larry Robinson becomes the fifth defenceman in NHL history to score 500 career assists when the Canadiens lose 6–4 to Toronto at the Forum.

JANUARY 10, 1985

Larry Robinson becomes the Canadiens' all-time leader in games played by a defenceman by appearing in his 891st game with the franchise, a 5–2 loss to the visiting Edmonton Oilers. The previous mark of 890 games was set by Doug Harvey in 1961.

JANUARY 12, 1985

The Montreal Canadiens announce their All-Time Dream Team on the occasion of their 75th anniversary: Jacques Plante in goal, Doug Harvey and Larry Robinson on defence, and Jean Béliveau, Maurice Richard, and Dickie Moore at forward.

FEBRUARY 15, 1985

Larry Robinson scores twice and adds an assist to become the second defenceman to score 150 goals with the Canadiens. The milestone comes in a 4–3 overtime win at Buffalo.

APRIL 11, 1985

Larry Robinson sets a team record for defencemen by appearing his 124th career playoff game, breaking the mark shared by Doug Harvey and Serge Savard. He reaches the milestone in a 5–3 win over visiting Boston in Game Two of the Adams Division semifinals.

APRIL 13, 1985

Larry Robinson sets a team record for defencemen with his 60th career playoff assist, breaking Doug Harvey's record. He reaches the milestone in a 4–2 win at Boston in Game Three of the Adams Division semifinals.

DECEMBER 19, 1985

Larry Robinson scores the only hat trick of his 20-year NHL career in a 5–4 loss to the Quebec Nordiques.

JANUARY 10, 1986

Larry Robinson sets a franchise record for defenceman by scoring his 167th career goal with the Canadiens in a 6–4 loss to the Rangers in New York. The goal breaks the record of 166 career goals set by Guy Lapointe in 1982.

MARCH 6, 1986

Larry Robinson becomes just the second defenceman in Montreal Canadiens history to get ten power-play goals in one season when he connects for the team in a 7–4 loss to the visiting St. Louis Blues.

MARCH 19, 1986

Larry Robinson becomes the first defenceman (and fourth player) to play 1,000 games with the Montreal Canadiens in a 6–4 loss to the Jets at Winnipeg.

MAY 24, 1986

Larry Robinson wins his sixth Stanley Cup championship as the Canadiens beat the Flames 4–3 in Calgary in Game Five of the final.

JUNE 10, 1986

Larry Robinson is named to Second All-Star Team for the third time in his NHL career.

DECEMBER 11, 1986

Larry Robinson becomes the fourth defenceman in NHL history to score 600 career assists when he assists on two goals in a 6–2 win against the New York Rangers.

DECEMBER 22, 1986

Larry Robinson scores the Montreal Canadiens' milestone 14,000th goal in franchise NHL history in a 4–4 tie against the visiting Pittsburgh Penguins.

FEBRUARY 16, 1987

Larry Robinson picks up four assists in the Canadiens' 7–3 win over the visiting Boston Bruins.

FEBRUARY 25, 1987

Larry Robinson scored the 800th point of his NHL career with an assist in a 3–3 tie against Chicago. Robinson becomes the fourth defenceman in NHL history to score 800 points.

APRIL 8, 1987

Larry Robinson scores a goal to become the first defenceman in Montreal Canadiens' history to accumulate 100 career playoff points. He reaches the milestone in Game One of the Adams Division semifinals, a 6–2 win over the visiting Bruins.

APRIL 24, 1987

Larry Robinson has three assists as the Canadiens win 7–2 against the Nordiques at Quebec in Game Three of the Adams Division final.

MAY 12, 1987

Larry Robinson ties a team playoff record for defencemen with four points (a goal and three assists) to lead the Canadiens to a 5–2 win at Philadelphia in Game Five of the Wales Conference championship.

MAY 14, 1987

Larry Robinson ties a team record for most assists in one playoff year with his 17th of the postseason in Game Six of the Eastern Conference final, a 4–3 loss to the visiting Flyers.

JANUARY 18, 1988

Larry Robinson picks up three assists to lead the Canadiens to a 6–4 win over the Oilers at the Forum.

APRIL 2, 1988

Larry Robinson has four assists as the Canadiens win 9–4 against the Buffalo Sabres at the Forum.

APRIL 6, 1988

Larry Robinson sets a Montreal Canadiens team record with his 98th career playoff assist, breaking Jean Béliveau's record. He reaches the milestone with two assists in a 4–3 win over the visiting Whalers in Game One of the Adams Division semifinals.

APRIL 9, 1988

Larry Robinson becomes the first player in Montreal Canadiens history to record 100 career playoff assists. He reaches the mark in a 4–3 win at Hartford in Game Three of the Adams Division semifinals.

MARCH 27, 1989

Larry Robinson becomes the first defenceman in NHL history to play 1,200 career games with one team and picks up three assists in the game when the Canadiens beat the visiting Bruins 5–2.

APRIL 5, 1989

Larry Robinson plays in an NHL record-tying 17th consecutive year in the playoffs when he appears in Game One of the Adams Division semifinals, a 6–2 Montreal victory over Hartford at the Forum.

APRIL 9, 1989

Larry Robinson sets an NHL record by appearing in his 186th career playoff game, a 4–3 overtime win over the Hartford Whalers in Game Four of the Adams Division semifinals. Robinson passes Denis Potvin, who had played 185 playoff games.

APRIL 21, 1989

Montreal's Pat Burns becomes the first coach in Stanley Cup history to win his first seven playoff games when defenceman Larry Robinson picks up three assists to lead the Canadiens to a 5–4 win at Boston in Game Three of the Adams Division final.

MAY 17, 1989

Larry Robinson becomes the second defenceman in Montreal Canadiens history to score 25 career playoff goals. He reaches the milestone in a 3–2 loss at Calgary in Game Two of the Stanley Cup final.

MAY 19, 1989

Larry Robinson becomes the first player in NHL history to play in 200 Stanley Cup playoff games when the Canadiens beat Calgary 4–3 in overtime in Game Three of the Stanley Cup final in Montreal.

MAY 21, 1989

Larry Robinson picks up his eighth assist of the 1989 playoffs, giving him 109 in his career and ranking him second on the all-time list for playoff assists. The Canadiens lose 4–2 to the Flames in Game Four of the Stanley Cup final.

JULY 26, 1989

The Los Angeles Kings sign free agent Larry Robinson to a three-year contract.

NOVEMBER 2, 1989

Larry Robinson's first goal as a member of the L.A. Kings comes in Boston and gives him the 896th point of his career, tying him with Brad Park for third place on the all-time scoring list for defenceman. Kings lose the game 5–4 to the Bruins.

NOVEMBER 11, 1989

The Kings defeat Montreal 5–4 in Larry Robinson's first game against his former teammates. It is his 18th game with the Kings and the 1,220th of his NHL career, placing him 20th on the all-time games-played list.

NOVEMBER 14, 1989

Larry Robinson has two assists in the first period of the Kings' 8–6 win over Calgary to move past Brad Park into third place on the NHL's all-time scoring list for defencemen.

NOVEMBER 22, 1989

Larry Robinson becomes just the second defenceman in NHL history to register 700 career assists as the Kings win 6–3 over the Blackhawks at the Forum.

DECEMBER 6, 1989

Larry Robinson scores the 200th goal and 900th point of his career as the Kings defeat the Vancouver Canucks 5–4. Robinson becomes the first NHL player to score 200 career goals without ever getting as many as 20 in one season.

JANUARY 30, 1990

Larry Robinson has a goal and an assist in the Kings' 5–2 victory over the New Jersey Devils to tie Bobby Orr for second place on the all-time points list among defencemen with 915. Denis Potvin was the all-time leader at the time, with 1,052.

FEBRUARY 1, 1990

Larry Robinson scores two points in a 7–4 loss to Chicago to break his tie with Bobby Orr and become the second-highest-scoring defenceman in NHL history.

APRIL 4, 1990

Larry Robinson sets a appears in the playoffs for a record-setting 18th consecutive year. The Kings trail 3–1 in the third period, but come back to beat the Flames 5–3 in Game One of the Smythe Division semifinals at Calgary.

APRIL 22, 1990

The Kings set a team playoff record for fastest two goals in a game when Larry Robinson and Todd Elik score just 11 seconds apart in the first period of Game Three of the Smythe Division final against Edmonton at the Forum. Kings lose 5–4 to the Oilers.

JANUARY 8, 1991

Larry Robinson becomes the 13th player in NHL history to appear in 1,300 regular-season games as the Kings beat the visiting Hartford Whalers 4–3.

OCTOBER 28, 1991

L.A. defeats the Detroit Red Wings, 4–3, at Joe Louis Arena for the 750th win in franchise history. forty-year-old Larry Robinson scores his first goal of the season with assists from 35-year-old Dave Taylor and 31-year-old Jay Miller, making the goal the product of 106 years of life experience.

MARCH 27, 1992

Larry Robinson records his 750th and final career assist in a 6–4 Kings loss at Winnipeg.

APRIL 14, 1992

Playing in the final regular-season game of his 20-year NHL career, Larry Robinson scores his final NHL goal (his 208th) and picks up his final career point (his 958th, ranking him fourth among defencemen in NHL history) in the Kings' 3–2 loss to Vancouver.

APRIL 18, 1992

Larry Robinson ties Gordie Howe's all-time record for most years in the playoffs when he appears in the postseason for the 20th time in the Kings' 3–1 loss to Edmonton. He also extends his own NHL record for consecutive playoff appearances.

JUNE 30, 1993

Larry Robinson, a member of six Stanley Cup championship teams, begins his NHL coaching career when he is named assistant coach of the New Jersey Devils.

JULY 26, 1995

The L.A. Kings name Larry Robinson as their new head coach, the 18th in team history. Robinson replaces Barry Melrose, who was fired late in the 1994–95 NHL season.

SEPTEMBER 11, 1995

The Hockey Hall of Fame announces its newest elected members: Larry Robinson, Fred "Bun" Cook, Bill Torrey, and Günther Sabetzki.

OCTOBER 7, 1995

Larry Robinson makes his NHL coaching debut as the Kings play their first NHL game of the season, a 4–2 opening-night win against the Colorado Avalanche at the Forum.

OCTOBER 21, 1995

The Kings' 3–2 overtime win at Pittsburgh gives them the best start (4–0–3) in the franchise's 28-year history. Coach Larry Robinson's streak is the third-best start by a new coach in NHL history.

OCTOBER 23, 1995

In a pre-game ceremony, Montreal GM Réjean Houle presents Kings coach Larry Robinson with a mural commemorating his playing days. Canadiens go on to win the game 6–3 over the visiting Kings, giving Los Angeles their first loss of the season.

NOVEMBER 20, 1995

The Hockey Hall of Fame officially inducts Robinson, Cook, Torrey, and Sabetzki.

DECEMBER 22, 1998

Larry Robinson earns his 100th NHL victory as a coach when Los Angeles wins 3–0 at Pittsburgh. Robinson becomes the fourth coach in Kings history to record 100 wins.

APRIL 19, 1999

One day after the end of the 1998–99 regular season, the Los Angeles Kings announce that they will not renew the contract of head coach Larry Robinson. Robinson finishes with a record of 122–161–45.

MAY 16, 1999

New Jersey Devils name Larry Robinson as an assistant coach.

MARCH 23, 2000

New Jersey Devils fire head coach Robbie Ftorek and name assistant coach Larry Robinson as his replacement.

MARCH 24, 2000

Larry Robinson wins in his New Jersey Devils coaching debut, an 8–2 win over the Islanders at Long Island.

JUNE 10, 2000

Larry Robinson wins his first championship as an NHL head coach and his seventh Stanley Cup title as the Devils win 2–1 at Dallas in Game Six of the final.

JANUARY 20, 2001

Larry Robinson records his 150th career coaching victory when the Devils record a 3–2 win over the visiting Atlanta Thrashers.

MARCH 2, 2001

Larry Robinson coaches his 400th NHL game as the Devils win 7–3 against the visiting Carolina Hurricanes.

JANUARY 27, 2002

The New Jersey Devils fire head coach Larry Robinson and name Kevin Constantine as his replacement.

FEBRUARY 25, 2002

New Jersey Devils name Larry Robinson as an assistant coach.

JUNE 9, 2003

New Jersey assistant coach Larry Robinson earns his eighth Stanley Cup championship when the Devils beat the visiting Mighty Ducks of Anaheim 3–0 in Game Seven of the final.

JULY 14, 2005

The New Jersey Devils name Larry Robinson as their head coach for the 2005–06 NHL season. Robinson takes over for Pat Burns, whose battle with cancer keeps him from returning.

OCTOBER 28, 2005

Larry Robinson records the 200th victory of his coaching career when the Devils extend their home unbeaten streak against Buffalo to 11 straight games (9–0–2) after a 3–2 win over the visiting Sabres.

NOVEMBER 3, 2005

Larry Robinson coaches the 500th game of his NHL career, a 4–2 loss to the visiting New York Rangers.

DECEMBER 19, 2005

Larry Robinson steps down as head coach of the New Jersey Devils. He is replaced on an interim basis by Devils general manager Lou Lamoriello.

JULY 25, 2007

The New Jersey Devils name Larry Robinson and Tommy Albelin as assistant coaches, joining John MacLean and Jacques Caron under new head coach Brent Sutter.

NOVEMBER 19, 2007

The Montreal Canadiens retire Hall of Fame defenceman Larry Robinson's number 19 sweater in a pre-game ceremony before a 4–2 loss to the visiting Ottawa Senators.

JULY 9, 2012

The San Jose Sharks name Larry Robinson as their new associate coach.

NORRIS TROPHY WINNERS AND FINALISTS THROUGH ROBINSON'S CAREER

	1	2
1972–73	Bobby Orr	Guy Lapointe
1973–74	Bobby Orr	Brad Park
1974–75	Bobby Orr	Denis Potvin
1975–76	Denis Potvin	Brad Park
1976–77	**Larry Robinson**	Börje Salming
1977–78	Denis Potvin	Brad Park
1978–79	Denis Potvin	**Larry Robinson**
1979–80	**Larry Robinson**	Börje Salming
1980–81	Randy Carlyle	Denis Potvin
1981–82	Doug Wilson	Ray Bourque
1982–83	Rod Langway	Mark Howe
1983–84	Rod Langway	Paul Coffey
1984–85	Paul Coffey	Ray Bourque
1985–86	Paul Coffey	Mark Howe
1986–87	Ray Bourque	Mark Howe
1987–88	Ray Bourque	Scott Stevens
1988–89	Chris Chelios	Paul Coffey
1989–90	Ray Bourque	Al MacInnis
1990–91	Ray Bourque	Al MacInnis
1991–92	Ray Bourque	Al MacInnis
1992–93	Brian Leetch	Ray Bourque

3	4	5
Brad Park	Bill White	Jacques Laperrière
Bill White	Barry Ashby	Börje Salming
Guy Lapointe	Börje Salming	Serge Savard
Börje Salming	Guy Lapointe	Serge Savard
Denis Potvin	Guy Lapointe	Serge Savard
Larry Robinson	Börje Salming	Guy Lapointe
Börje Salming	Serge Savard	Guy Lapointe
Jim Schoenfeld	Ray Bourque	Mark Howe
Larry Robinson	Ray Bourque	Rod Langway
Paul Coffey	Craig Hartsburg	**Larry Robinson**
Ray Bourque	Doug Wilson	Paul Coffey
Ray Bourque	Denis Potvin	Phil Housley
Rod Langway	Doug Wilson	Scott Stevens
Larry Robinson	Ray Bourque	Rod Langway
Larry Murphy	**Larry Robinson**	Paul Coffey
Gary Suter	Brad McCrimmon	Kevin Lowe
Al MacInnis	Ray Bourque	Steve Duchesne
Doug Wilson	Paul Coffey	Phil Housley
Chris Chelios	Brian Leetch	Paul Coffey
Chris Chelios	Brian Leetch	Paul Coffey
Phil Housley	Scott Stevens	Larry Murphy

ACKNOWLEDGEMENTS

So many contributed to the creation of *The Great Defender*, and Larry Robinson and Kevin Shea would like to extend thanks to the following:

Steve Bajinski, teammate with the Brockville Braves
Bill Barber, teammate with the Kitchener Rangers
Bob Berger, statistics research
Hersh Borenstein, Frozen Pond, Toronto
Larry and Rachelle Brehm, photos and research
Craig Campbell, Hockey Hall of Fame
Lloyd Davis, editor
Greg Donnelly, research
Margaret and Gerry England
Jordan Fenn, publisher, Fenn/M&S (Random House of Canada)
Mark Hebscher, research
Brian McFarlane audio files at the Hockey Hall of Fame
Nancy Niklas
Andrea Orlick, transcription
Paul Patskou, research
Jeannette Robinson
Paul Taunton, editor, Random House of Canada

As well as:

Hockey Hall of Fame (www.hhof.com)
Society for International Hockey Search (SIHR) (www.sihrhockey.org)
980CKGM Montreal Alumni (www.marcdenis.com/ckgm.asp)

BIBLIOGRAPHY

Béliveau, Jean, with Chris Goyens and Allan Turowetz. *My Life in Hockey.* Toronto: McClelland & Stewart, 1994.

Campbell, Ken. *Habs Heroes: The Greatest Canadiens Ever From 1 to 100.* Montreal: Transcontinental Books, 2008.

DiManno, Rosie. *Coach: The Pat Burns Story.* Toronto: Doubleday Canada, 2012.

Dryden, Ken. *The Game.* Toronto: Macmillan of Canada, 1983.

Fischler, Stan. *Hockey's 100: A Personal Ranking of the Best Players in Hockey History.* Toronto: Stoddart Publishing, 1984.

Geoffrion, Bernard, with Stan Fischler. *Boom-Boom: The Life and Times of Bernard Geoffrion.* Toronto: McGraw-Hill Ryerson, 1997.

Goyens, Chrys, and Allan Turowetz. *Lions in Winter.* Toronto: Prentice-Hall Canada, 1986.

Gretzky, Wayne, with Rick Reilly. *Gretzky: An Autobiography.* Toronto: HarperCollins, 1990.

Irvin, Dick. *Behind the Bench: Coaches Talk About Life in the NHL.* Toronto: McClelland & Stewart, 1993.

Irvin, Dick. *Now Back to You, Dick: Two Lifetimes in Hockey.* Toronto: McClelland & Stewart, 1988.

Irvin, Dick. *The Habs: An Oral History of the Montreal Canadiens.* Toronto: McClelland & Stewart, 1991.

Jenish, D'Arcy. *The Montreal Canadiens: 100 Years of Glory.* Toronto: Doubleday Canada, 2008.

Lefebvre, Robert. *Tales from the Montreal Canadiens Dressing Room.* New York: Sports Publishing, 2012.

Mouton, Claude. *The Montreal Canadiens: A Hockey Dynasty.* Toronto: Van Nostrand Reinhold, 1980.

Podnieks, Andrew. *Lord Stanley's Cup.* Bolton, Ont.: Fenn Publishing Company, 2004.

Robinson, Larry, with Chrys Goyens. *Robinson for the Defence.* Toronto: McClelland & Stewart, 1989.

Robinson, Larry, with Brian McFarlane. *Robinson on Defence.* Toronto: Collier Macmillan Canada, 1980.

Williams, Dave, with James Lawton. *Tiger: A Hockey Story.* Vancouver: Douglas & McIntyre, 1985.

Zweig, Eric. *Stanley Cup: 120 Years of Hockey Supremacy.* Toronto: Firefly, 2012.

The Hockey News: Greatest Teams of All Time

The Hockey News: Top 100 Players of All Time by Position

The Hockey News: Top 10, Counting Down the Game's Wonderful, Wild, Weird and Wacky!

INDEX